HUMAN RIGHTS IN TIBET

AN ASIA WATCH REPORT
FEBRUARY 1988

739 8th Street SE, Washington, DC 20003

36 West 44th Street, New York, NY 10022

ASIA WATCH COMMITTEE

The Asia Watch Committee was organized in 1985 to monitor and promote human rights in Asia. The Chairman of the Asia Watch is Jack Greenberg, its Vice Chairmen are Matthew Nimetz and Aryeh Neier, its Program Director is Eric Schwartz, and its Washington Representative is Holly Burkhalter. Asia Watch is affiliated with Americas Watch, Helsinki Watch and Human Rights Watch.

Cover design: Chuck Gabriel
Photo: ASUPI

Copies of this report are available from Asia Watch at $5.00 per copy.
    Asia Watch
    739 Eighth Street, SE
    Washington, DC 20003

TABLE OF CONTENTS

INTRODUCTION

The question of human rights in a minority area of the People's Republic of China is an inherently difficult one to research and address. With regard to Tibet, official sensitivity compounds the problem even further. The government's insistence that there is no human rights problem in Tibet, and its position that any discussion of the issue by foreigners constitutes unacceptable interference in China's internal affairs serve as serious obstacles to any examination of the question. As if to underscore this, the Chinese government has become increasingly vocal about the risk of damage to Sino-American relations should American politicians continue making negative comments about China's human rights record in Tibet.

In this atmosphere one should not be surprised at the extent to which mystery surrounds much of the information needed for any evaluation of human rights conditions in Tibet. As will become clear in the pages that follow, questions concerning political prisoners, population transfer, etc., are essentially hidden in secrecy. Gathering information on such subjects with regard to Tibet is a difficult undertaking but by no means should that force those concerned with basic human rights to designate Tibet *terra incognita* and to forego an attempt to bring conditions there into the light of scrutiny and open discussion. To do so would be to concede (as many governments insist) that human rights issues are internal matters with which the international community may not concern itself.

The basis of any organization's human rights work is the firm belief that human rights issues are of concern to the world community; and that it is the responsibility of those whose circumstances permit them a free voice to speak out on behalf of those whose rights are suppressed. Tibet is an unfortunate example of a place where suppression prevails, making international attention essential.

The prevailing political situation in the People's Republic of China and political suppression in Tibet do not allow us to monitor the human rights situation in that region as we might wish. The Chinese authorities do not allow detailed investigations of human rights abuses, and regulations formally prohibit foreign visitors from taking out materials that may be deemed harmful to the political interests of the Chinese state. As a result, some of the information on which Asia Watch must rely is anecdotal; present circumstances do not permit more comprehensive research. Asia Watch nevertheless has succeeded in gathering information on human rights in Tibet that indicates the seriousness of the situation. We have tried to pursue our concerns in a more wide-ranging manner as well: in October 1987, Asia Watch made a formal request to the government of the People's Republic of China, via its embassy in Washington, to send a delegation to Tibet to look further into the matters discussed in this preliminary report and to review them with responsible parties. Our request was not granted.

It should be pointed out that the Chinese government does, at times, veer away from a consistent stand against recognizing the importance of human rights issues in Tibet. Although it remains adamantly opposed to international dialogue when negative comment is involved, it goes to certain lengths to publicize positive comments, as reflected in some of the recent issues of China's English-language publications.

The report that follows is based almost wholly on information gathered by Asia Watch *in Tibet* and deals with a small number of severe problem areas. Information in this report originating with refugee sources outside Tibet is noted as such, and generally cited only when confirmed by observations inside Tibet. It must be emphasized that, by and large, this report only deals with abuses committed under the present government of the People's Republic of China, i.e., since 1980. Although it is common for Chinese authorities to ascribe such abuses to the chaos of the "Cultural Revolution" (1966-1976) and acts committed during the era of the "Gang of Four," Asia Watch finds that a pattern of serious human rights violations continues to characterize political and social life in Tibet today.

Though it is clear that Tibet's greater accessibility in recent years has made it possible to overcome some of the problems in examining the human rights situation, it must always be borne in mind that the danger to those Tibetans in Tibet who are willing to discuss basic human rights issues at any length is acute. One cannot overstate their courage.

TIBET AND THE TIBETAN QUESTION

Although documented contact between China and Tibet goes back at least to the sixth century, the modern-day debate about the historical status of Tibet takes the thirteenth century as its starting point, for it was at that time, so the present Chinese argument goes, that Tibet was drawn into the map of China. The basis for the Chinese argument is the conquest of both realms by the Mongols, even though Mongol domination of Tibet and China began and ended at different times. The extent to which Tibet was made specifically subordinate to the Yuan dynasty (1270-1368), the dynastic apparatus through which the Mongols ruled China, seems vague at best. The Mongol empire was a world empire, and though there is no doubt that Mongol domination extended into Tibet, there seems little basis for maintaining that the Mongols appended Tibet to China.

The succeeding dynasty, the ethnically Chinese Ming dynasty (1368-1644), clearly recognized that Tibet was quite distinct and separate from China. In an early document the first Ming emperor referred to Tibet as a foreign state, in language that was unequivocal. There were no serious attempts during the Ming dynasty to make Tibet a part of China. When the succeeding Qing dynasty had the official history of the previous dynasty compiled, the monograph on Tibet was placed in the section set aside for "Western Regions," and included the imperial domains of Tamerlane, hardly integral parts of China.

The question of Tibet's relationship to the Qing dynasty (1644-1911) is more problematic. The Qing, like the Yuan, was a conquest dynasty. Its Manchu rulers established an empire that had clear lines separating the administration of Tibetans, Mongols and Chinese; and governing their relations to the throne. What complicated the situation was the intense Sinicization of the Manchus in China during the eighteenth and nineteenth centuries, ultimately resulting in a people who considered themselves distinct from their Chinese subjects but who nevertheless had largely lost the most telling of distinctions: their own language. This metamorphosis was visible enough in China, but ironically did not really effect the administrative structure binding Tibet to the throne in a Manchu empire.

Tibet was incorporated into the Manchu dominions by various stages in the eighteenth century; at century's end Tibet was clearly under the control of the Manchu throne. The administrative arrangements under which this control existed were, however, quite separate from those pertaining to China. Chinese officials and Chinese provinces had no part in the governing of Tibet, save when in the eighteenth century large portions of eastern Tibet were detached from the jurisdiction of the Dalai Lama's government and placed under that of provincial and court officials. Today those portions of eastern Tibet still remain outside the modern Tibet Autonomous Region (TAR) although the cultural, religious and ethnic links between the Tibetan populations remain.

Under the Qing, Manchu officials supervised the Dalai Lama's government. The administrative apparatus for the management of Tibetan affairs was, during most of the dynasty, a bureau known as the "Court of Colonial Affairs." Its mandate clearly seems to have been the management of the court's dealings with areas that were *not* integral parts of the empire's Chinese realms. Thus it dealt with areas in the west, those places whence envoys came to court via overland routes: not simply areas such as Mongolia and Tibet, but (until the second half of the nineteenth century) Czarist Russia as well. There is a rather tragic irony inherent in the fact that as the Manchus became more Sinicized in China, far away in their realm's outer dominions these structures which held the Manchu empire together as a Manchu Empire, though already a creaking anachronism, were still in place. In the latter decades of the Qing there did appear plans (some realized, some not) to render some of the realm's Inner Asian areas into parts of China by simply making them Chinese provinces. Implicit in such actions was the notion that such an administrative change was the key to the integration of the outer dominions into China. Neither Tibet nor Mongolia were made into Chinese provinces, though preliminary military moves that were certainly aimed in that direction had been undertaken with regard to Tibet.

When Manchu rule collapsed in 1911, both Tibet and Mongolia acted on the assumption that the structure linking them in one realm was defunct, and established themselves as independent states. We may take note of the fully parallel status of both lands under Manchu rule. Further complications about Tibet's position arose from the question of the extent to which China was seen to be the heir to all the Manchu realms. Mongolia escaped the implications of this problem. Tibet did not.

The U.S. did not recognize Mongolia until this past year. Certainly the geo-political factor of Mongolia's alignment with the Soviet block had much bearing upon this. To a great extent, however, recognition for Mongolia was witheld for the same reason it was never accorded to Tibet in the years after 1911: American desires not to offend China's Guomindang rulers, both during the Republican period and later on after the Guomindang had fled to Taiwan.

In the years following the Qing collapse, the Chinese republic was able to lay claim to all of the Qing dominions without the issue ever coming to a head. To some extent this was surely because the Republic of China could do little more than claim these areas. The territory of the present TAR was wholly under the rule of the Dalai Lama's government, with no regard shown for Republican claims. The Mongolian People's Republic, under Soviet protection, was likewise beyond China's reach, as was much of Xinjiang for a good part of the pre-1949 period.

The establishment of the People's Republic of China (PRC) in 1949, and the flight of the Guomindang Republican government to Taiwan, marked the eventual end of Tibet's independence. It should be understood that when Tibetans raise this issue they are conscious of a time in the recent past — i.e., prior to 1951 — when the territory of the present Tibet Autonomous Region was in fact independent of any Chinese rule. Moreover, whatever one may think about the justice or viability of Tibetan claims to independence, it ought to be acknowledged that the Chinese historical view of the situation is not necessarily accepted by Tibetans; it is surely not the point of view that Tibetan activists bring with them to the political dialogue.

The history of Tibet as part of the PRC is likewise controversial. By 1949 the PRC was in control of most of those areas of the Tibetan Plateau that had been detached by the Manchus from the government of the Dalai Lamas. On October 7, 1950 troops of the People's Liberation Army crossed the *de facto*

7

line of control of the Dalai Lama's government and, shortly thereafter, defeated the small and ill-equipped Tibetan Army. The Dalai Lama's government was forced to negotiate with the Chinese central government and to accede to the Agreement on Measures for the Peaceful Liberation of Tibet, which was signed on May 23, 1951.

This did not put an end to tension between Tibet and China. Tibetan areas inside and outside the territory of the present TAR were treated quite differently. In the latter regions, which were placed under Chinese provincial administration, social and political policies rooted in the Chinese experience were followed that precipitated an armed rebellion in the early 1950s. It should be borne in mind that the social and economic situation, as far as the ratio of people to workable land was concerned, was directly opposite in Chinese and Tibetan regions; Tibetan territories were very sparsely inhabited, allowing for a certain degree of flexibility and mobility as far as those on the lower rungs of society were concerned. The Chinese insistence, on the basis of the universals of Marxist analysis, that Tibetan society should be categorized as "feudal," and ordinary Tibetans as "serfs," has only served to obfuscate the situation. Tibetan society was assuredly not modern, but it cannot be construed as feudal in the classic sense. Adding to the confusion is the somewhat neocolonial twist that the official Chinese position has given to discussion of the Tibetan issue. A rather dubious litany of "feudal" tortures that were routinely inflicted upon the "serfs" is adduced as one of the aspects of Tibetan society from which the natives had to be saved. Presently, PRC officials rebuff concern over the issue of human rights in Tibet with the retort that any who are critical of present Chinese practices are only trying to restore the "feudal serf system" in Tibet.

The rebellion began in the eastern areas of the Tibetan plateau, outside the bounds of the present TAR, but it eventually spilled over into that area, culminating in an uprising in Lhasa in 1959. The Dalai Lama fled to India along with many other Tibetans, ultimately creating an exile community that presently numbers over 100,000. For a short time the Chinese government made use of the Panchen Lama, another important Buddhist hierarch, but he fell into disfavor and disappeared until the late 1970s (since which time he has actively cooperated with the Chinese government). The crushing of the rebellion led to the application in Central Tibet (the area of the present TAR) of the social and economic policies that had been applied in the east. It also led to a massive number of imprisonments. It is said that most of those sent off to prison in the wake of the 1959 uprising in Lhasa never returned. Those who did return seem to have spent close to twenty years in prison; most were released only in the late 1970s.

On September 1, 1965, Central Tibet was constituted as an autonomous region (the TAR). Not long thereafter the Cultural Revolution commenced, precipitating further havoc and destruction in Tibet, beyond what the strife in the 1950s had wrought. Strictly doctrinaire Maoist policies were implemented in Tibet that produced extreme economic and social damage. Only in 1979/1980, with the consolidation of power in the hands of those allied with Deng Xiaoping, did a more liberal era begin. The Panchen Lama and several other Tibetan figures were restored to favor at this time and given central government appointments.

The present period in Tibet is indeed a more open and relaxed one than those that preceded it in the recent past. There is a good deal of respectable cultural and scholarly activity going on in Tibet; monasteries have been reopened and religion is once more in evidence. The State's more provocative ideological premises (such as the inevitability of the disappearance of religious and national characteristics and differences) are no longer given the wide publicity that they received in more radical periods. At the same time, it is known that the Chinese central government has been carrying on negotiations over the Tibetan issue with representatives of the Dalai Lama. Nevertheless, in spite of such welcome signs of openness, a large store of Tibetan resentment against China remains. It is estimated by Tibetan exiles that well over one million Tibetans died from unnatural causes in the thirty years between 1950 and 1980, all stemming from Tibet's incorporation into the PRC. It is of course impossible to verify such a figure under present conditions. Nevertheless, the numbers must be very high; it is rare to meet a Tibetan who hasn't lost at least one relative in the turmoil of those years. There are other pieces of evidence that show that the period must have been very bloody. Population statistics reveal a disproportionate dearth of males in Tibet, particularly in the eastern part of the plateau, where fighting in the 1950s was said to have been extremely heavy.* A booklet marked "secret" and published in Lhasa on October 1, 1960 by the political department of the Tibetan Military District states with reference to the aftermath of the Lhasa uprising: "From last March up to now we have already wiped out (*xiaomie*) over 87,000 of the enemy."** In addressing the issue of Tibetan deaths during the period Chinese spokesmen have responded disingenuously, as if the million-plus figure referred only to the territory of the TAR. They mock the figure and maintain that the TAR had only 1.1 million people in 1951 (which can only be an estimate) and that it now has close to two million; and that a loss of more than a million lives in the region over three decades is therefore impossible.*** At the same time, however, Chinese population estimates from 1953 and 1964 show a loss of more than 200,000 people from the PRC's total Tibetan population, making the Tibetans the only nationality in the PRC with a population of one million or more to experience a population decline during the intervening years.****

Against this background there remains an obvious reserve of resentment against China on the part of many Tibetans. Unfortunately this is exacerbated by what Asia Watch considers the systematic violation of certain basic human rights. It has become clear that despite liberalization in some areas, political imprisonment, torture, and discrimination are also characteristic of the current situation in Tibet, specifically in various towns and cities on the Tibetan plateau. This disregard for human rights is very close to the surface of political, social and religious life in Tibet. Although the government of the PRC maintains that this is wholly an internal affair, Asia Watch strongly believes that

---

*   See map 40 ("Sex Ratio") in Oxford University Press's The Population Atlas of China, (Oxford, 1987).

** Xizang xingshi ho wenwu jiaoyu di jiben jiaocai (Lhasa, 1960), p. 6.

*** "Suowei 'baiwan Zangmin bei sha' shizai huangmiu," Renmin ribao, October 8, 1987.

**** Zhang Tianlu, "Growth of China's Minority Population," Beijing Review, June 18, 1984, p. 23.

human rights are a universal issue, and that the human rights situation in Tibet is an extremely serious one and warrants international attention.

* * *

The Tibetan Plateau is by and large where most of the Tibetan population has traditionally lived. The present-day TAR covers only a portion of the plateau, however. Today there are a number of other, lower-level autonomous units with significant Tibetan populations that are contiguous with the TAR, but which remain within the jurisdiction of neighboring Chinese provinces. Aside from the TAR, we may list these units as follows (giving their names as transcribed from Chinese): the Guoluo Tibetan Autonomous Prefecture, the Haibei Tibetan Autonomous Prefecture, the Hainan Tibetan Autonomous Prefecture, the Haixi Mongol-Tibetan Autonomous Prefecture, the Huangnan Tibetan Autonomous Prefecture, and the Yushu Tibetan Autonomous Prefecture, all in Qinghai Province; the Aba Tibetan-Qiang Autonomous Prefecture, and the Ganze Tibetan Autonomous Prefecture, both in Sichuan Province; the Gannan Tibetan Autonomous Prefecture, and the Tianzhu Tibetan Autonomous County, both in Gansu Province; and the Diqing Tibetan Autonomous Prefecture and the Muli Tibetan Autonomous County, both in Yunnan Province. The TAR was proclaimed on September 1, 1965. The other units were established in the 1950s.

As in the rest of the PRC, these Tibetan areas have both government and Communist Party organs. It is generally conceded that real power rests with the party. Local party leadership is generally held by a Chinese (or non-Tibetan) party first secretary, while a Tibetan is usually assigned to the position of chairman or head of the local people's government. The 1984 Law on Regional National Autonomy for Minority Nationalities (article 17) stipulates as much.* Presently the chairman of the local people's government of the TAR is Dorje Tsering (Rdo-rje tshe-ring/ "Duoji Caireng"), a Tibetan, while the local party's first secretary is Wu Jinghua, a non-Tibetan from outside the region.

---

*   Zhonghua renmin gongheguo minzu quyu zizhifa (Lhasa, n.d. [= 1984?]), p. 8.

11

Within Tibet, police work and the maintenance of order are the responsibilities of the local branches of the Public Security Bureau (PSB). Similarly, local Tibetan areas also have branches of the People's Procuratorate and the People's Court to deal with investigations, trials and sentencing. The Law on Regional Autonomy for Minority Nationalities (article 46) stipulates that in autonomous nationality areas leading officials in these organs are to be drawn from the ranks of the local autonomous nationality. The law (article 47) also emphasizes the use of local nationality languages in investigative and trial documents and procedures.* The extent to which Tibetans and the Tibetan language are employed as prescribed by the law is presently unclear. The meager information available seems to indicate the continuing primacy of the Chinese language and Chinese personnel in these areas.

---

*   Zhonghua renmin gongheguo minzu quyu zizhifa (Lhasa, n.d. [= 1984?]), pp. 15-16.

THE EXERCISE OF FREEDOM OF RELIGION, SPEECH AND ASSEMBLY IN TIBET

The moderation that may be said to characterize some of the policies implemented in the TAR during the present decade does not extend into the realms of free political discourse or full religious freedom, in spite of governmental insistence to the contrary.

Religion in Tibet may be considered a private affair only to the extent that believers keep their faith within carefully prescribed limits. Those limits can only be intended to hamper the propagation and unbounded reinvigoration of religion in Tibet. Religious institutions are not independent, but are linked to external organs such as offical Buddhist organizations and "management boards for cultural relics" established in diverse localities. Religious practice is accorded protection by both the 1982 Chinese Constitution (article 36) and the more recent 1984 Law on Regional National Autonomy for Minority Nationalities (article 11). The latter stipulates:

> The autonomous organs of regional national autonomy protect the freedom of religious belief of citizens of all nationalities. No state organs nor public organizations can compel citizens to believe in or not to believe in religion, nor can they discriminate against citizens who believe in religion and citizens who don't believe in religion. The state protects normal religious activities. No one can use religion to carry on activities that disrupt public order, harm the physical well-being of citizens, and impede the national educational system. Religious bodies and religious affairs are not to be subject to foreign domination.*

Terms such as disruptions of public order, foreign domination, etc. leave a great deal of room for subjective interpretation; and in Tibet government

---

*   Zhonghua renmin gongheguo minzu quyu zizhifa (Lhasa, n.d. [= 1984?]), pp. 5-6.

controls exerted over religious practice and religious institutions go well beyond these vague limits. Those limits are not set down openly in order that they might be discussed and analyzed, but according to Tibetans are made known to those who need to know them. It would appear, nevertheless, that there is some variation, depending on locality, as to the degree of control exerted by the local authorities.

* * *

Since the beginning of the 1980s the Chinese government has allowed Tibetans to begin reconstructing and renovating a number of the temples and monasteries that had been severely ravaged or wholly destroyed in the preceding decades. The government has also publicized its role as a benefactor in this work. Nevertheless, the number of religious institutions being restored represents only a small percentage of the total number destroyed. Evidence indicates that in many areas the decision as to whether a particular building will be restored rests with the local authorities, and these authorities do not all act uniformly. It is said that in a few areas the local authorities have granted believers permission to renovate a larger number of religious structures than in others. Such areas are by all accounts few and the reasons behind this divergent policy may be based on a number of factors. Tibetans will state that the decision to renovate a monastery or not is essentially linked to tourism, and to the desire of local government and party officials to boost an area's revenues from the tourist trade. It is also likely that officials in some regions are simply lenient in such matters. In Qinghai and Gansu provinces, there has been a degree of monastic reconstruction in some areas that seems to go beyond the mere requirements of tourism. The A-mdo peoples resident in the region are appreciative of such moves, but are not wholly free of skepticism about the motives. Some feel that this is simply a superficial move intended to assuage the religious sensibilities of the politically less sophisticated and, also, to remove some of the monastic ruin that is a reminder of the violence of past Chinese policies. For the most part though, the renovation and reconstruction of monasteries is not freely permitted, and the role of tourism in the present wave of renovation is undeniable.

According to Tibetans, the number of temples and monasteries being rebuilt would be much greater if permission from local authorities (and in some cases from the Central Government) were not required. In many cases it has been necessary for Tibetans to persist in requests to rebuild particular institutions. In some, there have been arrests as a result of unauthorized building, probably the most well-known example being Ganden (Dga'-ldan) monastery, located some forty kilometers outside Lhasa. Early attempts to rebuild Ganden were met with arrests,[*] until the government finally stopped trying to halt its reconstruction and simply looked the other way. Progress was very slow. Then in July, 1987, it was announced with fanfare that Ganden was to be rebuilt.[**] No explanation or expression of regret about the previous obstructionist actions and arrests accompanied the news. Tibetans in Tibet maintain that in cases where they have been able surreptitiously to rebuild or to restore ruined monasteries or temples, the Chinese government has taken the credit once the restoration is completed. More to the point, they also maintain that funds publicly announced by the Chinese government to be set aside for such work are grossly exaggerated. According to them, the bulk of the money comes from Tibetans; that is, from local believers and pilgrims. Likewise, much of the labor is donated. Some funds from the Chinese government do reach these projects, but they represent only a small fraction of what is required.

Strict financial regulations govern the management of monasteries in Tibet. The Jokhang, the "Central Cathedral" in Lhasa, has been permitted to

---

[*] Such was the case according to a number of informed sources in Tibet. Phuntsog Wangyal (Phun-tshogs dbang-rgyal), a member of the second delegation sent to tour Tibet by the Dalai Lama's government-in-exile, visited Ganden in the summer of 1980 and reported in a long statement prepared for Tibetans living in Darjeeling, India, that Tibetans attempting to rebuild parts of Ganden were subjected to financial harassment; i.e., being forced to pay higher rents and fees and the like. At the same time the delegation was officially told that it was the Chinese themselves who were rebuilding Ganden. "Bod-nang gzigs-skor thengs gnyis-pa'i sku-tshabs tshogs-pa'i khongs Ing-lan Bod-rigs tshogs-pa'i tshogs-gtso Phun-tshogs dbang-rgyal lags-kyis Rdor-gling khul ser-skya mi-mang-rnams-la Bod-nang-gi gnas-tshul dngos-yod gsal-bsgrags bskyang-pa," Bod-mi rang-dbang, September 26, 1980.

[**] "Yellow Hat' Monastery to be Rebuilt," The China Daily, July 8, 1987. Compare with the preceding note.

15

maintain only 1,000 Renminbi (RMB; US $1 = RMB 3.75) on hand at any one time. All other funds must be on deposit in the government bank. According to Tibetans the activities of the temple are readily controlled by the state through its decisions to allow money to be dispensed by the bank. Monks receive salaries of 50 RMB a month (for which it must be attested that they have worked diligently). This salary is paid out by the bank from funds that were originally collected from offerings by visitors. Tibetans also maintain that Chinese officials have access to such bank accounts on the pretext of using the money for temple repairs. Tibetans we interviewed claim that the government maintains an unacceptable level of control over religious affairs in this and in other ways.

* * *

The monastic vocation is also a matter in which government authorities have a say. In recent years more lenient policies have allowed the monastic ranks to grow considerably, at least compared to what they were a decade ago. Nevertheless entry into the clergy is not solely an individual decision, nor simply one between a believer and the monastic establishment. The government regulates the numbers of monks in various monasteries and has the power to refuse entry. In the Lhasa area young boys are said by Tibetans to be allowed to become novices without much obstruction. Once a child is older, however, and wishes to become a fully ordained monk, strict approval from the authorities is required. Without that no salary or financial support will be provided.

Tibetans maintain that the controls which the Chinese have imposed on the monastic system inside the TAR and in the Tibetan areas outside it afford the government the ability to supervise monastic affairs closely. In all monasteries, at least one person must act in a leadership capacity as a liaison with the authorities and therefore has the responsibility to keep them informed about what may be happening in the monastery. Not surprisingly those persons are often mistrusted by their own fellow monks.

* * *

Tibetans in Tibet state that there are clear limits on their right to practice Buddhism. They say that generally they are only accorded the freedom to perform certain rituals and to make public displays of some aspects of religious faith. Thus they may perform prostrations in the vicinity of various sacred objects or sites. Many Tibetans believe that this, like the reconstruction of monasteries, is linked to tourism. The sight of Tibetans prostrating themselves in streets and in temples is not simply picturesque, however; it also creates the impression that the PRC grants full religious freedom to Tibetans and that, to all appearances, religious practice in Tibet is little more than the performance of bizarre acts of abasement rooted in superstition. Offical tolerance of such activities is intended to be seen by tourists and visitors who are otherwise unfamiliar with Tibetan culture as a manifestation of religious freedom in Tibet.

Nevertheless, it is obvious that limits on religious practice are stringently maintained by the authorities. As one would expect, it is forbidden to offer prayers publicly for the Dalai Lama. Monks do this privately, however. Reportedly, permission from the authorities is required for any large-scale ceremony in several monasteries; a number of such ceremonies have been permitted in recent years, but Tibetans deny that the situation is in any way comparable to what it was in the past or would be if religious affairs were not government controlled. The Great Prayer Festival associated with the Tibetan New Year is probably the best example of a large ceremonial and ritual event that has been given official sanction. In February, 1986, it was reinstituted (in a somewhat truncated form) after a twenty year government ban and has subsequently received publicity in Chinese publications,* perhaps with an eye to its tourism potential. Such concerns also seem to underlie the restocking of certain monasteries with religious statues and images that are not properly sanctified. These images are meant to replace the extraordinary number that were destroyed or taken to China over the last several decades. Those that were placed in the Jokhang, and which constitute the majority of images now there, were installed under the supervision of a Chinese Muslim official and are said by Tibetans to be devoid of the ritual requisites.

Propagation of the Buddhist faith is another area in which Tibetans feel they are denied religious freedom. There is a prohibition on religious

---

*   See "Lasa qidao da fauhi," Renmin ribao, March 30, 1986.

teachings, it appears, in most of Tibet. In the Lhasa area, a handful of venerable monks are allowed to give teachings to large groups of lay people. This group includes Gen Lamrimpa Ngawang Phuntshog (Rgan Lam-rim-pa Ngag-dbang phun-tshogs) of Drepung ('Bras-spungs) monastery and Geshe Senge (Dge-shes Seng-ge) of Sera (Se-ra) monastery. They are exceptional figures, however, and they are strictly enjoined from any sort of incorrect political utterances.

The restriction on the propagation of Buddhism in Tibet appears to an outside observer to be intended to keep religion in check, lest it become a powerful emotional force (with the potential for manipulation) among the Tibetan people in general and an ideological rival to the state's Marxist ideology among the Tibetan intelligentsia. Prompted by such concerns, the state has attempted to co-opt the instructional functions of the monasteries and the clergy has been unable even to debate the questions raised by this practice. Tibetans we interviewed state that they are allowed no right to speak out against such a government move.

In 1983, a government supervised religious school, the "Tibet Academy of Buddhism," was opened at the Nechung (Gnas-chung) monastery, just below Drepung. Reportedly, the school did not stay open very long. According to Tibetan exile accounts, the school was opened precipitously, and little Buddhist discipline and study was provided for the students who were selected to go there. The accounts claimed that most students drifted away, and the school closed.[*] Current Chinese reports make no mention of this and state that the school is now open and operating. It is maintained that "any young man at the age of 18, who is in good health and has acquired at least middle school education can volunteer to enter the academy with his family's consent." Enrollment is officially pegged at 170.[**]

---

[*]   "Chos-dad rang-mos zer-ba'i ngo-bo ther-'don," Shes-bya, April, 1986, p. 10.

[**]   Wu Naitao, "Lamaism Flourishing in Tibet," Beijing Review, October 26-November 1, 1987, p. 29.

18

In 1987, the central government launched its own Tibetan Buddhist religious school, located in Beijing. The institute opened on September 1 and according to the Chinese press, forty-two incarnate lamas were chosen for the institution's first class (the curriculum takes one year to complete). As if to underline the political supervision and influence of the central authorities, the Panchen Lama (who is credited with creating the school) said that it would train high religious figures who "ardently love the socialist motherland."* It must be assumed that the aim of the academy at Nechung is similar. One may read into this the government's intent to take Buddhist education out of the hands of the monasteries in order to control it ever more firmly.

Many Tibetans believe that the government purposely blocks the teaching and propagation of Tibetan Buddhism in a manner compatible with the standards of monastic instruction. They maintain that the religious and philosophical curricula that were provided in the educational environment of the monasteries have been forcibly suppressed and that there is nothing they can do to reinstitute them. Should a member of the clergy begin organizing a rigorous curriculum for the education of monks, comparable to what existed in the past, he would be inviting stern measures and possibly severe punishment from the authorities.

* * *

Freedom of written and spoken expression is another area in which there are restrictions that warrant concern. At present the suppression of free speech via harsh measures in Tibet appears to relate largely to political issues, particularly those issues surrounding the status of Tibet, the return of the Dalai Lama, and the presence of large numbers of Chinese in Tibet. The authorities control book, magazine and newspaper publication and thus there is no free access to the media. Nevertheless, the present variety and diversity of publications in the Tibetan regions of the PRC is quite remarkable when compared with the situation prior to 1979/1980. Today one finds publications containing works on history, literature, language, society, and other subjects, as well as short stories,

---

*   "Zhongguo Zangyuxi gaoji Foxue yuan ji jiang kaixue," <u>Renmin ribao</u>, August 31, 1987.

19

and classical Tibetan works. This is not to say that there are no political or ideological limits applied to what one may write in such publications; there are, but that still has left a good deal of leeway for those who are permitted to write and publish. The writings on religion that do appear, however, for the most part are not of the sort that could be effective in propagating the faith. They are, rather, largely academic writings (e.g., dealing with the history and social structure of Tibetan Buddhism, or with the classification of works in the corpus of Tibetan Buddhist literature). There does seem to be an adequate supply of works available in Tibet that advocate atheism.

Tibetans do note that a number of classical religious works have begun to appear in modern editions from various nationality presses in the PRC. In addition, several of Tibet's traditional printing centers, where books are printed on long unbound leaves from woodblocks, have been able to resume their printing activities and once more to produce numerous volumes of classical Tibetan works, including important Buddhist texts.

* * *

Restrictions on freedom of expression and freedom of assembly in Tibet are stringently applied to all political utterances and actions. Tibetans emphatically state that the influx of Chinese into Tibet now affords the PSB in Tibet and its local branches the opportunity to maintain more effective surveillance over the populace. Thus, Tibetans in Lhasa made a point of noting that during former U.S. president Jimmy Carter's visit to the Tibetan capital in June 1987, a number of people intended to give him written appeals concerning the human rights situation in Tibet and the Tibetan desire for independence (such appeals have often been thrust into the hands of Western tourists). This proved impossible, however, as it was clear to those who were intending to get close to the former president that his public movements were being carefully observed by agents of the PSB. These agents wear no distinguishing uniforms and outwardly dress to resemble many of the ordinary Chinese migrants who have set up stalls and tables for commerce in various parts of Lhasa or who are engaged in other work.

Chinese are not the only people who work for the PSB, but they do constitute the majority of bureau workers according to Tibetans in Lhasa. They make it all but impossible for Tibetans to give vent to any political sentiments at variance with China's Tibet policy. The events of September and October 1987 amply reflect this. The demonstration that precipitated the harsh repression and bloodshed of early October was a nonviolent march around the Jokhang led by 20 to 30 monks on September 27. The participants, by all accounts, did little more than shout slogans calling for Tibet's freedom and independence as they circled the Jokhang and headed down "People's Road" (Mi-dmangs lam in Tibetan; Renminlu in Chinese) to the Tibetan local government compound. This nonviolent expression of strongly-held political sentiments brought down arrests and beatings upon the march participants. Their incarceration led to the larger demonstrations on October 1, when a police station was stormed and burned.* Subsequent accounts from Chinese sources make it clear that the nonviolent expression of political opinion that questions or denies the legitimacy of China's claim to Tibet can produce serious consequences. The participants in the September 27 march were said by Ngapo Ngawang Jigme (Nga-phod Ngagdbang 'jigs-med), a prominent Tibetan member of the National People's Congress in Beijing, to have mounted a "serious political incident....they will be dealt with according to the law."** Such statements are cause for deep concern, as the legal situation of people accused of creating such "incidents" can be bleak. If they are deemed to be counter-revolutionaries, the penalties may be severe. The most well-known Tibetan dissident, Geshe Lobsang Wangchuk (Dge-bshes Blo-bzang dbang-phyug), was sentenced to more than eighteen years in prison solely on the basis of his writings and his refusal to recant his opinions and beliefs. That much was already known to western observers several years ago. In October, however, members of the Chinese central government's State Nationalities Commission for the first time publicly defended the incarceration of Lobsang Wangchuk in official publications, although the crimes that he was

---

* These events received much attention in the Western press during October 1987. They are discussed at greater length in a later chapter.

** "Ngapoi Condemns Incident" FBIS-CHI-87-189, September 30, 1987 (quoting a Xinhua dispatch of September 29), pp. 46-47.

said to have committed cannot be described as anything other than writing and speaking out for what he believed in:

> [Lobsang Wangchuk] put up reactionary notices on two occasions in 1979 and 1980, concocting the so-called "history of Tibet's independence" and inciting separatist activities. So he was arrested again on October 26, 1981 under China's Criminal Law.*

The case of Lobsang Wangchuk will be discussed in greater detail in the next chapter. For his crimes of conscience and his refusal to back down from his position on the status of Tibet he was subjected to beatings and other abuses in prison, even in the face of strong foreign concern about his case. Asia Watch believes that his treatment directly contradicts the Chinese government's public statements professing respect for human rights in Tibet. It is clear that prohibitions on free political expression and assembly in Tibet are the norm. Regulations relating to public assemblies announced in Lhasa on October 9, leave little room for doubt on this point:

1. These regulations are being promulgated....for the purpose of ensuring the lawful exercise of the citizen's right of assembly....
2. Organizers of assemblies and processions must personally submit a written application to the city Public Security Bureau 5 days beforehand. These applications must explain the purpose of the assembly or procession, the number of participants, the time, the location, and the route, as well as the names, professions, and addresses of the organizers.
3. ...No applications that violate the Constitution and the law will be approved.

---

* "Religion, Crime and Citizen's Rights," Beijing Review, October 26-November 1, 1987, p. 25. The article is said to consist of an interview with unnamed members of the State Nationalities Commission conducted by Beijing Review. A similar interview published in Liaowang (overseas edition), October 12, 1987, contained the same question on Geshe Lobsang Wangchuk. The answer varied slightly, with the officials stating "There does not exist the problem of 'cracking down on political dissidents.'....We regret to say that some people have used the case of such a persom to stir up confusion." See "Official Views Xizang Issue, Dalai Lama," FBIS-CHI-87-198, October 14, 1987, p. 18.

5. ...People are forbidden to engage in illegal activities aimed at splitting the motherland or sabotaging national solidarity....

7. Assemblies and processions for which approval has not been granted are illegal and are totally banned. The organizers and directors of such events, and those who pay no heed to admonition, must be punished according to law.*

* * *

Political opinion that runs counter to China's official stand on the Tibetan question is expressed publicly in leaflets and wall posters. The PSB is vigilant with regard to such expressions of dissident sentiments. According to Tibetan sources, when written tracts or posters calling for Tibetan independence appear, the PSB acts quickly to uncover their source. In the spring of 1987, during Saka Dawa (Sa-ga zla-wa; the fourth month of the Tibetan calender, and a period of increased religious activity as the traditional dates for the Buddha's birth, enlightenment, and death all fall within it), posters demanding freedom and independence for Tibet appeared on walls behind the Potala, the Dalai Lama's residence. Since a small Tibetan quarter of Lhasa lies just below the Potala, small groups gathered to read them before they were torn down. PSB officials also were aware of these posters; in ordinary civilian clothes they joined groups reading them and began to make inquiries as to their origin. When that yielded no information, a watch was put on area residents who had been seen reading the posters. Searches are often carried out in instances such as this, when the PSB is seeking the source of what it deems counter revolutionary or separatist written materials. That in itself can be a rather terrifying experience for those questioned, as the penalties for being implicated in such activity may be imprisonment and brutal treatment, as will be discussed below.

It is not simply leaflets or tracts originating in Tibet that put one in danger of arrest. Mere possession of the flag of the traditional Tibetan government is also a serious offense. Even more serious is possession of political materials originating among the Tibetan exiles in India. It is maintained by

---

*   "Assemblies, Processions Rules," FBIS-CHI-87-197, October 13, 1987, p. 36 (quoting a Radio Lhasa broadcast of October 10, 1987).

Tibetans in Tibet that possession of such materials automatically implicates one as a spy for the Dalai Lama. With the opening of the Nepal-Tibet border, it has become possible for Tibetans in India to visit relatives in Tibet and (with certain restrictions) for Tibetans in Tibet to visit India. As a result such political materials from India have appeared in Tibet, and arrest is a serious danger for those who possess them.

POLITICAL IMPRISONMENT IN TIBET

Conditions of Arrest and Imprisonment

It is difficult to separate the issue of political imprisonment in Tibet from those of freedom of speech and assembly. As noted already, there is one urgent issue around which almost all political activity seems to be centered: the question of Tibet's status and the related questions concerned with the possible return of the Dalai Lama and the withdrawal of the Chinese from Tibet. Tibetans in Tibet maintain that all political arrests under the present regime are ultimately linked to the expression or manifestation of opinion in any way seemingly sympathetic to the position that China's presence in Tibet is unjust.

* * *

As already mentioned, the PSB maintains effective surveillance over the Tibetan population in most major towns and cities. When an individual is suspected of speaking out against Chinese rule in Tibet or in favor of Tibetan independence he or she is watched ever more carefully. Note is taken of where the person lives, what he or she looks like, and a special surveillance is set up. The person's residence is also likely to be searched. If leaflets or other materials calling for Tibet's freedom or independence are found, an arrest is made immediately. Possessing a representation of the old Tibetan flag is considered an equally serious crime. When arrests take place, they are usually carried out secretly, in the middle of the night. As one Tibetan put it:

> The gatekeeper* is told to be quiet and not to lock the door.
> ...he is told that [the PSB] will be coming. They come at around
> 1:00 or 2:00 [in the morning], quietly, when everyone is asleep....Then they take the person away....and the interrogation
> is carried out....

---

*   Most residences in the Tibetan quarter of Lhasa and other Tibetan cities are arranged around closed courtyards.

25

After the arrest is made, the person is taken for interrogation to a PSB branch bureau. In Lhasa these branches are located in various parts of the city, and the questioning begins immediately, while most of the populace sleeps. According to an observer in Tibet whom we believe to be both informed and credible:

> After they arrive [at the PSB] interrogation is done: "Where did you go during such-and-such a month? What work did you do?....How much time off did you have? How many days did you work?"....The answers are compared with information already obtained from the person's workplace....If the information doesn't match the person is harshly told: "You haven't told the truth, you've lied. Where have you gone? Think hard. Where did you go on the day [illegal] posters were put up? What did you do?..." These are the sorts of questions asked in interrogation. When they know that the person in question is the one who has put up posters, ones stating that Tibet is independent...or [if it is a question of leaflets] when they have gotten information about others involved in the distribution of leaflets, then the person is taken from the interrogation room and brought to court for sentencing.

All of this takes place in secret. Some Tibetans in Tibet insist that court proceedings follow hard on the heels of the interrogation, as in the description above. It appears from other materials, however, that there may be a lapse of some time (months, perhaps even years) between arrest and the official handing down of the sentence. Throughout that time, however, the prisoner remains incarcerated, with whatever sentence that was determined administratively at the time of interrogation remaining in effect. The official determination of the sentence may be simply a pro-forma confirmation of the decision already made.

It is the interrogation that has already determined the guilt of the person arrested. It is obvious that there is no place in the prevailing legal system for any sort of outside assistance, representation, or other concessions to allow the accused to mount a defense; this, at least, is the situation so far as political offenses in Tibet are concerned. The official secrecy and silence surrounding almost all political cases is in effect from the time of arrest to the time of release. It is such that in one instance, the case of Jampa Kalsang (Byams-pa skal-bzang;

26

his case is discussed in greater detail below), it is known that even the prisoner's family was left uninformed about his whereabouts for some days, until the arrival of PSB officials to do a further search of their quarters made it clear that he was in custody. There are no public announcements made concerning political crimes. It is generally believed that the prisoner's family members are put under routine surveillance after an arrest.

The interrogation at the PSB branch is carried out by the People's Procuratorate of the local municipality or district, while the court proceedings are held under the auspices of the People's Criminal Court of the same area. According to Tibetans the rights of the accused extend no further than being allowed to acknowledge the crimes with which he or she is charged. It is forbidden for the prisoner to speak up and dispute the charges.

Torture is not spared in the interrogation of political prisoners, according to informed and credible observers in Tibet. It is a means for obtaining information and for dealing with recalcitrant prisoners. As one person described it:

> If one speaks forcefully, if one gives an account of Tibet as being independent, they apply cattle prods [in Tibetan, *glog-gi rgyug-pa*; literally "electric batons"]. One's feet are shackled, one's arms are shackled. The whole body trembles and one can't speak.

The use of cattle prods in Tibet unfortunately corresponds to other descriptions concerning the use of these instruments on prisoners elsewhere in the PRC.* During the most recent clashes in Lhasa, the PSB use of cattle prods also figures in accounts of violence against protesters.

It is generally believed that in recent years (i.e., since approximately 1980) sentences for political crimes have become lighter. Whereas previously the possession of leaflets or the pasting up of posters asserting Tibet's right to independence and professing antipathy to the Chinese presence in Tibet might bring a sentence of twenty years (or death), sentences now generally amount to

---

* See the Amnesty International report, <u>China: Torture and Ill-treatment of Prisoners</u> (London, 1987), pp. 14-15.

three to five years. Nevertheless, the authorities reserve the right to increase such sentences later on if it is believed that the prisoner is being obstinate in holding to counter-revolutionary ideas. That was the case with Geshe Lobsang Wangchuk, whose original sentence in 1981 (when he was 67 years old) was three and a half years. That was ultimately augmented and reached a total of more than eighteen years, a sentence that ensured that he would never again be allowed to move freely among other Tibetans.

* * *

The mistreatment of political prisoners does not end with interrogation and sentencing. Such prisoners are subjected to various forms of abuse and torture during their imprisonment. Geshe Lobsang Wangchuk, probably the most well-known example, was left with little use of his hands as a result of this sort of mistreatment. Beatings in prison can take on a regular, routine air. The secrecy which marks the initial stages of arrest continues during imprisonment. Tibetans note that there are restrictions on talking throughout most of the prison day. As a result, political prisoners inside the same prison may be largely unaware of each other's presence. Nevertheless, it is the belief of many that the political prisoners are often singled out for particular abuse by the prison authorities. It is believed that this generally comes toward the end of the prison day, when discussions on the day's work are held under the gaze of the prison authorities. These discussions can often lead to graver "struggle sessions" in which those who show ingratitude or resistance toward the party and the country are beaten. Invariably it is the political prisoners who suffer.

* * *

Life and the daily routine in a Tibetan prison under China's present leadership has been described to Asia Watch as follows:

> We are required to work eight hours a day; we are given only enough food to keep us from dying. There is very little to eat in our meals....We get momo [dumplings] in the morning, at noon, and in the evening....We work breaking rocks, making paper packing for cement. There are quotas, and we have to make three or four thousand sheets [a day]. We have to fold the paper by hand and the hands get badly bruised. There is a fixed size for the rocks [after they are broken] sixty to eighty

pieces have to be made a day....We eat in the morning at 7:30... and work starts at 8:00. We have momo and plain tea in the morning. The momo are "trin momo" [i.e., plain bread rolls, not the stuffed dumplings usually associated with the term "momo"]. At work we do our tasks separately and without talking. We are not allowed to speak to one another. If we do, they use cattle prods on us and yell at us. We work as if we were mute. Work continues up to 12:30. At the noon meal there are [plain bread] momo and boiled cabbage....There are ten people per room [in the prison] and boards on either side for five people....Someone pours plain tea and we each take momo from the center of the room. We eat our own food and remain quiet. We're not allowed to talk even if not eating. Speaking is not permitted. There is a group leader who is placed among us and he watches us to see what this one or that one says....

After lunch we resume work at 3:00. We work from 3:00 until 7:00....Illness is no excuse for not working. You have to work. You're not allowed to be sick. At 7:00 work is finished and we return to eat. After eating a meeting is called. [We are asked:] "Today, how much work did you do?" Each room in the prison has ten people, twelve at most. They constitute a group unit. The questions of how much work one has done are asked within the group....We are given political instructions about following the example of what Chairman Mao, China, and the people have done...about how good the Chinese Communist Party is, how well the people are doing, that this is our tomorrow, that our [old] thoughts will be destroyed and we will be new people. There is always a meeting after eating in the evening. Every month there is an execution meeting at which all the prisoners are gathered together to watch. Guns are loaded and the condemned person is brought in. All the prisoners are gathered together and are told: "You had better be good. You had better love the Communist Party. This person's life is forfeit." We draw a political lesson from this.

Struggle sessions are held [in prison]...and people are beaten fiercely. People in the group unit are told: "You speak! You speak!" The person to be "struggled" against is placed in the middle and is told that he has not done well, that he has said

29

such and such. If he argues and fights back he is shackled, hands and feet...and placed in a dark room, [still] shackled. Two prisoners are placed in an outer room to watch him. Outside...PSB people are stationed. The prisoner can be in that room for one, five, or six months. Thieves and murderers are in the prison too, but political prisoners are treated worst of all....They don't want to kill them outright, as that would be scandalous in much of the world, so they treat them very badly. There are also some Chinese in the prison, mostly thieves, but some are murderers...Actually, we can't have contact with each other, so there is no way to really know how many are political prisoners. The entire process [of imprisonment] is carried on secretively.

After [execution] meetings are over, we return to our own rooms for discussion....We're told about what will happen if we don't follow the Communist Party...that the person executed reaped the fruits of not following the Communist Party....After this everyone has to write down his opinion about what had just happened...and state that he will follow the Communist Party. If one states that he will not follow the Communist Party, that it is bad, his hands and feet are immediately shackled....All have to say that they will be good. There is no liberty to speak freely.

The day is over at 8:30-9:00, when the doors are locked....Talking is not allowed. The group leader watches us to see who speaks....At midnight, 1:00, or 2:00, people come to check on whether anyone is talking or not.

Political prisoners are not placed together [in living quarters]....[Common criminals] are placed in their rooms with them. They [the political prisoners] are not permitted to make contact with each other....Trouble does break out between the political prisoners and the thieves and murderers [in the same rooms] in the evenings. There is fierce fighting. If one is not a political prisoner one isn't immediately placed in the dark room. For something very grave one's feet and hands are shackled. The thieves and murderers don't know who is a political prisoner....All of those in charge....ask questions of the others...."What has he done? What has he been looking at? What has he said?" They thus use the other nine or ten people [in the room]. At meetings [the group leaders] don't use political reasons to provoke beatings of political prisoners. There are many people [at meetings] and they don't know [that one is a political prisoner]; they use other [nonpolitical] reasons to provoke them into beating [political prisoners]....All those in charge know who the political prisoners are.

One has no religious rights in prison....Recitation of the *mani* is not allowed....A small number of people have minor visitation privileges. They can have a visitor on one day of each month. Political prisoners, because they are...such trash...are denied this. Now they can have visitations once every three or four months...for only two minutes. There is a PSB worker nearby to listen to all that is said....We have no idea about what is happening outside. Only family members can visit.... Visitors have to make themselves clearly known to the authorities: "Where are you from? Who are you going to see? What is your [district] committee? Where is your residence?...."

There is torture in prison....When one is questioned, if good answers are not given cattle prods are used...one is severely beaten....In the winter one is forced to kneel on ice...the pants are rolled up, one is bound tightly and one's [bare] knees are on the ice for an hour....[In prisons] in sparsely populated areas [i.e., away from the cities] one is beaten very often. One is beaten with rifle butts.

* * *

It is distressing, but no longer surprising to find that torture is part of the prison routine in Tibet. Torture and violence against prisoners in China proper has even received attention in Chinese publications.* Unfortunately, the sensitive nature of the Tibetan issue has caused the Chinese authorities to maintain a strict refusal to acknowledge improprieties against prisoners in Tibet.

---

* See the Amnesty International report previously cited, China: Torture and Ill-Treatment of Prisoners.

Political Prisoners

Tibetans in Tibet maintain that prisons in all the main Tibetan regions, both inside and outside the TAR, confine political prisoners. In the Lhasa region prisons are known to be located at Drapchi (Grwa-bzhi), Sangyip (Gsang-yib), Gutsa (Dgu-rtsa), and Tse Gungthang (Tshal Gung-thang). Political prisoners are sometimes sent further away from their Central Tibetan home areas to isolated prisons and labor camps in Kong-po, Pu-mi, and other areas. In addition, small, local prisons are said to be scattered throughout the TAR.*

It is extremely difficult to ascertain the number of political prisoners in the TAR and in neighboring Tibetan areas. The secrecy surrounding the process of political imprisonment — the fact that almost no part of that process, from first arrest to final release from prison, is openly and publicly acknowledged — hinders attempts to be accurate with regard to the number currently held as political prisoners throughout the Tibetan plateau. Only during October 1987 (*after* the demonstrations in Lhasa had erupted, resulting in the arrest of at least scores of Tibetans for political offenses) did the Chinese authorities attempt to address foreign concerns on the question. They said that there were only two labor camps and one prison in the TAR and that they held a total of only 974 prisoners; and among those prisoners only 28 were guilty of "counter-revolutionary crimes" (i.e., political offenses).**

The figure of 28 for the total number of political prisoners in the TAR must be rejected. The recent unrest alone has resulted in the incarceration of far more than 28 Tibetans for political offenses. Nevertheless, strict governmental secrecy on the question of political imprisonment in Tibet (accompanied by studied dissimulation on the issue to the outside world) leave us with only the

---

* Regarding prisons on the Tibetan plateau and their populations up to the early 1970s (when they still held a number of prisoners who had been arrested in 1959), see Phyi-lo 1965 lor Bod rang-skyong-ljongs btsugs-pa nas 1973 bar Bod nang-gi gnas-tshul-la zhib-'jug zhus-pa'i phyogs-bsdoms snyan-zhu (Dharamasala, 1974), pp. 94-96.

** "Official Views Xizang Issue, Dalai Lama," FBIS-CHI-87-198, October 14, 1987, p. 18, quoting the October 12, 1987 overseas edition of Liaowang.

vaguest idea of the number of Tibetan political prisoners both inside and outside the TAR.

Even before the events of late September and early October 1987, Tibetans in Tibet generally estimated the number of political prisoners in Tibet to be perhaps scores in the Lhasa area and several thousands throughout the TAR. Considering the serious nature of political offenses in Tibet, and the strict measures which the authorities are empowered to take against them, we must assume that there is a considerable number of Tibetan political prisoners currently incarcerated and, regrettably, incarcerated under conditions similar to those described above.

* * *

The following Tibetans are among those believed by Asia Watch to have been imprisoned for political offenses. The first case is that of Geshe Lobsang Wangchuk. Lobsang Wangchuk is now believed to have died in prison on November 4, 1987 (even though this has been denied by the Chinese authorities).* His case is particularly important because it brings into focus a number of issues relating to political imprisonment in Tibet. Moreover, as a result of the international attention he obtained, Geshe Lobsang Wangchuk was the only political prisoner incarcerated under the present regime whose case has been commented upon by PRC authorities.

Geshe Lobsang Wangchuk

A short biography of Geshe Lobsang Wangchuk that has appeared in the Tibetan exile press provides us with some basic biographical details.** He was born in the lesser A-mdo region under the jurisdiction of Nag-chu in Central Tibet on November 2, 1914 (the 15th day of the second month of the Tibetan Wood Tiger Year). At the time of the 1959 uprising in Lhasa, Lobsang Wangchuk was in Nag-chu and considered to be one of the region's religious

---

*   "Death of Leading Tibetan Activist Denied," FBIS-CHI-87-225, November 23, 1987, p. 22, quoting an Agence France-Presse dispatch of the same date.

**   "Dpa'-bo'i brjid-nyams-kyi mig-dpe'i rdo-ring rgan Blo-bzang dbang-phyug," Shes-bya, May, 1987, pp. 3-6.

leaders. In 1962, he was imprisoned and sentenced to 10 years. In 1963, he was transferred to Drapchi prison in Lhasa, where his health was said to have suffered as a result of numerous "struggle sessions." In 1970, as the term of his imprisonment was nearing its end he was attached to a work team and sent out to break rocks. In time, following completion of his sentence, he was made to work variously in a brick factory in Nethang (Snye-thang), near Lhasa, and in farming and herding. It is said that the work and working conditions differed little from that which he would have had to do in prison. In the period following the ascendancy of Deng Xiaoping, he surreptitiously wrote and pasted up posters rebutting what was then being published by the Chinese-controlled printing houses about Tibet, its people, history and current conditions. He was given the task of editing medical texts for publication by the Tibetan Medical Center in Lhasa. By this time, however, the Chinese were said to have become suspicious of him. On December 3, 1981, he was rearrested and sentenced to three and a half years in prison.

From other sources Asia Watch has learned that Lobsang Wangchuk had authored a book (or possibly a booklet; the length of the work is not clear) entitled "A History of Tibetan Independence." At the time of his last arrest, the work was being readied for secret distribution in and around Lhasa, and possibly elsewhere. It is reported that his audacity in preparing such a work and in standing by the opinions in it was largely responsible for the particularly harsh treatment he received in prison.

Geshe Lobsang Wangchuk's original sentence of three and a half years was extended by an additional fifteen years during the time of his imprisonment as a result of his refusal to confess the error of his views during various criticism meetings and interrogations. In October, 1983, it was reliably reported that Lobsang Wangchuk was among a number of Tibetan prisoners who were scheduled to be executed as part of a mass anti-crime campaign then being mounted throughout the PRC. Groups in several countries organized protests on his behalf and this pressure may have helped to save him at that time. The case of Geshe Lobsang Wangchuk was subsequently taken up by Amnesty International which noted in a recent report that it had received word that he had been kept shackled, hands and feet, from September 1983 until February, 1984.*

During the last two years or so, Geshe Lobsang Wangchuk was reported to have been held in Drapchi prison. He is said to have been beaten on several occasions, the excuse being his inability to perform the hard labor required of prisoners; this accords with testimony we have obtained that non-political pretexts are often found for beating and mistreating political prisoners. All reports maintain that Lobsang Wangchuk adhered to nonviolence. According to one Tibetan in Tibet, while in prison he is said to have told the prison authorities that the Tibetan issue should be settled through debate and verbal disputation; that if no one in the TAR was competent to argue the question with him then the central government should send someone to do so. Perhaps apocryphally, he is reported to have said that he would offer his life to the Chinese side should it win. What, he asked, would China offer should his arguments vanquish their position?

Early in 1987, Lobsang Wangchuk was reported to be losing his sight as a result of beatings. Then the following report from Tibet was received by Asia Watch:

> On February 24, [1987,] at 7:00 in the evening, Lobsang Wangchuk, age 70 [sic], being unable to perform manual labor, was not only beaten, but had his hands twisted by two [Tibetans working at Drapchi Prison], Political Instructor Tashi (Bkra-shis) and Team Leader Paljor (Dpal-'byor), beyond normal limits.

* * *

As a result of this, Lobsang Wangchuk was no longer able to use his hands. Ironically (or pointedly), he was then given a certificate — after a doctor had seen him — excusing him from work. Thereafter, his contact with others was cut off, save for the most minimal interaction with those who brought him food, etc.

---

* China: Torture and Ill-Treatment of Prisoners, p. 10.

Amnesty International reported that Lobsang Wangchuk died on November 4, 1987. This has been denied by Chinese authorities, but nevertheless the report is generally believed to be true. Perhaps the most distressing aspect to the case of Lobsang Wangchuk is the fact that the international attention focused on him seems to have done little to ameliorate his situation. Only in 1987 did the Chinese address the concerns of many people outside China regarding his imprisonment and the grave abuses to which he was subjected. The Chinese response on these matters is discussed below. In any event, it is absolutely clear that the authorities under whom Geshe Lobsang Wangchuk was imprisoned felt that they could act with impunity in mistreating him; that the secrecy under which political imprisonment is carried on in Tibet would guarantee the absence of any need to respond to Tibetan or international concerns for his safety and well-being.

Jampa Kalsang

Jampa Kalsang (Byams-pa bskal-bzang), believed to be in his early 40s, married and the father of three sons, was a resident of the Klu-sgug area of Lhasa prior to his imprisonment. He was arrested on September 26, 1986, according to an article in *Shes-bya*, the monthly Tibetan-language magazine published by the Tibetan Government-in-Exile, based in Dharamsala India.* Most of the details about his arrest recounted in the article have been confirmed by Tibetans in Tibet. Jampa Kalsang did construction work in Lhasa. In accord with the policy of secrecy as regards political imprisonment, nothing was known about what had happened to him until some days after his arrest. It is said that even his family was given no indication as to what had befallen him. On September 29, 1986, PSB officials showed up at his home to conduct a thorough search. Only then, it is said, did it become clear that he was in fact being detained.

The article in *Shes-bya* stated that the primary motivation for arresting Jampa Kalsang was that he had served as the patron for religious teachings held earlier at Drepung. Tibetans in Tibet maintain, however, that the PSB linked

---

* "Nyes-med Bod-mi 'dzin-bzung byed mtshams-'phral-du 'jog dgos," Shes-bya, December 1986, pp. 3-4.

him to printed materials advocating independence for Tibet that were distributed at Drepung. *Shes-bya* also states that a copy of the Tibetan-language edition of the Dalai Lama's autobiography was found in his home, a fact which (if true) is believed to be sufficient to implicate him as a "spy" for the Dalai Lama and the Tibetan exile authorities. Jampa Kalsang was sentenced to three years in prison. He is presently said to be held in Gutsa prison in Lhasa.

Panden Gyatso

Panden Gyatso (Dpal-ldan rgya-mtsho) is a monk from Drepung. Originally from Shekar (Shel-dkar), a district in Tsang (Gtsang) along the main road to Nepal, he is 54 years old. Panden Gyatso had been imprisoned previously in 1960 for participating in the 1959 rebellion and was not released until 1975. Afterwards he became a monk at Drepung.

In August, 1983, a group of Beijing-based foreign correspondents from thirteen countries went to Tibet on an arranged visit. Panden Gyatso is said to have passed on to some of them a written appeal for Tibet's independence and to have spoken to others about the hopes of Tibetans for the return of the Dalai Lama. Reportedly, he told them that Tibetans await the Dalai Lama's return "as the thirsty await water." He is also believed to have told them that the Dalai Lama should only return when the Chinese are gone, for only then could his safety be guaranteed. During this period a number of Tibetans passed similar appeals to the visitors, and the resulting press reports reflected the sense of unhappiness with Chinese rule in Tibet that the journalists perceived. In the aftermath, the PSB carried out a massive sweep among Tibetans in Lhasa, according to Tibetans still there, arresting those suspected of having expressed such sentiments to the journalists; Tibetan exile sources claimed that 500 Tibetans were arrested at the time.* Among those arrested was Panden Gyatso.

---

* See "Visting Journalists See Signs of Resistance," Tibetan Review, August 1983, p. 4; and "500 Tibetans Arrested in Lhasa," Tibetan Review, September 1983, p. 4; Typical reports on the visit include Michael Weisskopf, "Separatists Keep Up Struggle for Free Tibet," The Washington Post, August 13, 1983; and Jeff Sommer, "Tibet Longs for Dalai's Return," Newsday, August 15, 1983.)

According to information obtained by Amnesty International, Panden Gyatso was arrested in Lhasa on August 26, 1983, and, on April 19, 1984, was sentenced to eight years imprisonment and two years deprivation of political rights for distributing counter-revolutionary propaganda. The PSB claimed to have found in his diary on the day of his arrest a "reactionary letter" meant for the Dalai Lama. It was said to have expressed reactionary and anti-socialist sentiments. In addition, he was accused of having pasted up posters in Lhasa on March 9, 1982 calling for Tibetan independence.

Dawa

Dawa (Zla-ba) is also referred to by Tibetans as Shol Dawa because he comes from the Shol (Zhol) district of Lhasa, just below the Potala Palace. He is in his 50s and was arrested in late August, 1985. According to Tibetans in Tibet he was found by the PSB to have leaflets in his home appealing for the independence of Tibet. His arrest came in preparation for the September 1, 1985 celebrations meant to mark the 20th anniversary of the establishment of the TAR. Reports of his arrest appeared in the Tibetan exile press, but no mention was made of his having leaflets.* This is not the first time that he has been incarcerated, and he is reportedly cut off from all outside contact. It is maintained that he was given a 7 year sentence. During the course of his imprisonment so far, he is said to have been frequently shackled for long periods of time. He is presently believed to be held in Drapchi.

Kalden

Kalden (Skal-ldan) is a member of the mixed Tibetan-Nepalese community based for the most part in Lhasa. This community is largely a commercial one whose members enjoy trading privileges that were granted to them several generations ago by the Tibetan government. His age is uncertain. He

---

* "Behind the Recent TAR Celebrations," Tibetan Review, October-November, 1985, p. 4; and "Bod-mi sa-ya drug ni zhum-pa med-pa'i gdong-len 'thab-'dzings-pa zhig yin-pa," Shes-bya, October, 1985, p. 12.

was arrested in 1982 after passing a letter to a foreigner stating that Tibetans want independence. He is believed to be held in Drapchi.

Jamyang

Jamyang ('Jam-dbyangs) is from a family now living in Lhasa, but originally from the Khams area of eastern Tibet. Prior to his arrest, he was a postal worker. His age is not known, but it is believed that he was accused of having taken a letter that was being directed to a Tibetan PRC agent in Dharamsala (the seat of the Tibetan government-in-exile) and rerouted it so that it went to the Tibetan exile authorities instead. He was arrested in 1985 and is believed to be held in Drapchi.

Thubten

Thubten (Thub-bstan) is Jamyang's brother. Prior to his arrest, he was serving in the local Tibetan militia. It is believed that he was accused as an accomplice of his brother in the act of rerouting a letter to the Tibetan exile authorities and was arrested and imprisoned at the same time. He too is reported to be held in Drapchi.

Kunsang-tse

Kunsang-tse (Kun-bzang-rtse) is the name of an aristocratic family in Lhasa. One of the family's members is reliably reported to have been under arrest since September 1985, the time of the celebrations of the 20th anniversary of the founding of the TAR. His proper name is not known (he was referred to only as Kun-bsang-rtse'i *sras*, literally "Kunsang-tse's son"), but he is said to be 31 years old and was a middle school teacher until his arrest. He is accused of being a spy for the Dalai Lama, a charge that is believed to indicate that he probably had printed political materials from Dharamsala in his possession. He too is believed to be held in Drapchi.

* * *

Asia Watch did not obtain specific information on another prisoner, Thubten Kelsang Thalutsogentsang, who has been adopted by Amnesty International as a prisoner of conscience. Nevertheless, his case warrants attention too. According to Amnesty International, Thubten Kelsang Thalutsogentsang was imprisoned in 1981 for shouting slogans in favor of Tibetan Independence. He is believed to be held in Sangyip prison.*

* * *

The demonstrations that occurred in Lhasa on September 27, October 1, and October 6, 1987, were harshly suppressed by the Chinese authorities. The course of those events is described in another section of this report; in addition to what happened at the demonstration, one should bear in mind that reports which have reached Asia Watch paint a rather grim picture of their aftermath. Word has come that there have been a considerable number of arrests, as well as some executions, in the Tibetan quarters of Lhasa. Although these events are discussed in greater detail below, it is important to note that they fall within the context of a system of sharp and often brutal repression of political dissent that has characterized China's administration of Tibet for several decades. The demonstrations of September and October 1987 were wholly unexpected; the response unfortunately falls within an established pattern.

---

* For more details on this case see the description given by Amnesty International in China: Violations of Human Rights (1984), pp. 48-49.

POPULATION TRANSFER AND RELATED PROBLEMS

Movement of Chinese Into Tibet

The movement of large numbers of Chinese on to the Tibetan Plateau and into the TAR is the object of vociferous differences of opinion. Points of contention include questions about the actual figures for the Tibetan and Chinese populations on the Tibetan Plateau; Chinese encouragement of migration into Tibet; and the very question of whether the movement of Chinese into Tibet is a valid object of foreign concern and criticism.

It has been suggested that the movement of large numbers of Chinese into Tibet violates international law because it contravenes legal norms regarding occupied territories.* This position postulates acceptance of the premise that Tibet is an occupied country and that China's presence there is as an occupying power. Although this report does not concern itself with Tibet's legal status, Asia Watch believes that the transfer of Chinese into Tibet merits serious scrutiny and comment, due to its impact on Tibetan life and culture. Beyond this, there is evidence of strong patterns of discrimination against Tibetans arising out of the growth of the Chinese population in Tibet. That is reason enough to examine this population movement.

* * *

The extent of Chinese settlement in the TAR and on the Tibetan Plateau is felt in a number of ways. There is, however, little consensus about the number of people that this movement affects, Tibetan or Chinese. It is the position of Tibetans in exile, and of many sympathetic non-Tibetans, that there are presently 7.5 million Chinese on the Tibetan Plateau as opposed to 6 million

---

*   Michael C. van Walt van Praag, <u>Population Transfer and the Survival of the Tibetan Identity</u> (New York, 1986).

41

Tibetans. The former figure is at best difficult to substantiate, while the latter one must be rejected.

It is impossible to gauge accurately the extent of Chinese migration to Tibet. As with a number of other issues relating to Tibet, the sensitive nature of the matter precludes an accurate count being permitted by the Chinese authorities. In addition, when Tibetan exiles refer to Chinese migration into Tibetan areas outside of the TAR (e.g., Tibetan territories in Qinghai) they generally claim small areas that have substantial Chinese populations — populations that in some cases have lived in those regions for centuries. To some extent this derives from the rather inaccurate belief that Chinese provincial lines follow Tibetan ones (e.g., in the case of Qinghai, that the entire province falls within the Tibetan region of A-mdo). The number of Chinese actually dwelling in Tibetan areas must be well below the 7.5 million figure.* In a similar way, the figure of 6 million for the number of Tibetans on the plateau cannot be accepted either. The figure itself has actually become more symbolic than literal, as if Tibet's population had remained unchanged for at least twenty years.** That is highly unlikely, not least because of the violence and bloodshed Tibet endured during that period. The most recent Chinese census (1982) gave the Tibetan population of the PRC as 3.87 million, of whom 1.82 million lived in the TAR. By now it is believed that the total Tibetan population has passed the 4 million mark. The Tibetan population of the TAR is said to be 1.93 million.***

---

*   To get an idea of the extent of Tibetan habitation, one may look at the outline of Tibetan territories delineated in the recently published map of autonomous national minority areas in the PRC: Zhonghua renmin gongheguo minzu zizhi difang fenbu tu (Fujian, 1986).

**   The figure 6 million for the Tibetan population has been used at least as early as 1967, when it was cited solely as an estimate by Tsepon W.D. Shakabpa in Tibet: A Political History (New Haven, 1967), p.6.

***   On the population of the TAR see "Dalai Lama 'Slander' About Xizang Refuted," FBIS-CHI-87-189, September 30, 1987, p. 12, which quotes from a Xinhua dispatch of the same day. On the Tibetan population in general, according to the 1982 census, see Zhang Tian-lu, "Growth of China's minority population," Beijing Review, June 18, 1984, pp. 22-26 and 30.

Controversy is unavoidable when one deals with the most basic element of this issue, the number of Chinese who have moved into Tibet. In addressing that question, PRC authorities have steadfastly maintained during the last few months that they amount to only 73,000.* This figure, however, must be rejected out of hand. Even a casual visitor to Lhasa can see that there are at least that many in the capital alone; in fact the actual figure for the city may be a good deal higher. Like the issue of political imprisonment, that of Chinese migration into Tibet is one that is covered by a purposeful secrecy arising out of political sensitivity.

A semi-official work published in Lhasa in December, 1984 gave the total population for the city as "about 50,000-60,000."** Although there is no ethnic breakdown, that figure would seem consciously to exclude Lhasa's Chinese residents. In contrast, an unofficial brochure published by the tourist bureau in Lhasa in July, 1986, gave the city's population as 110,000.*** The latter figure would seem to be based on the common-sense observations of its compilers; it is generally estimated that Lhasa has a population of somewhat more than 150,000, most of whom are Chinese. In spite of the obvious size of Lhasa's population, however, official publications are clearly unwilling at this time to address in earnest questions about the number of Chinese resident anywhere in Tibet.

Although we can say with confidence that there are more than 60,000 inhabitants in Lhasa, and that there are more than 73,000 Chinese in Tibet, we cannot hazard a reasonably reliable estimate of the total number of Chinese in the TAR. Political conditions in the region do not allow us to carry out the sort of survey that might clarify the figures. Nevertheless, there can be little doubt that Chinese constitute the majority in most of the centers of population concentration. In most large towns and cities in the TAR, and in neighboring

---

*   See "Dalai Lama 'Slander' About Xizang Refuted," FBIS-CHI-87-189, September 30, 1987, p. 12.

**   "Xizang zizhiqu gaikuang" bienxie zu, Xixang zizhiqu gaikuang (Lhasa, 1984), p. 43.

***   Chen Ran, ed., Summits in Tibet [Xizang zhi zui] (Lhasa, 1986), pp. 7 and 16.

Tibetan areas, Chinese predominate, and sometimes seem to be double the Tibetan population (as appears to be the case in Lhasa). By contrast, there seem to be few Chinese settled in the non-urban areas of the plateau, deep in nomadic or remote agricultural areas; though it is reported that Chinese settlement is pushing into non-urban Tibetan regions outside the TAR, especially in Gansu province and along the eastern edge of Qinghai province.

* * *

Why is this settlement occurring, and why now? There are several reasons that quickly come to mind: the central government's desire to integrate Tibet more firmly into the PRC; its desire to better secure the region, both politically and militarily; and its intention to modernize and develop the region. There are undoubtedly other reasons that may be considered as well, but this report is not the proper forum from which to embark upon a detailed analysis and background discussion of these reasons. Asia Watch's interest in the issue derives from the fact that as the PRC implements its decisions regarding Chinese migration into Tibet, important questions of cultural, civil and political rights in Tibet are knowingly ignored. It has already been noted, for instance, that the influx of Chinese into Lhasa has made surveillance far easier than it was previously. From the point of view of the Chinese government then, the demographic changes that have occurred in the Tibetan capital are helpful in the maintenance of political security in the city. But this means a severe cost is being paid by Tibetans who desire to express nonviolently opinions and sentiments at variance with the government's line. By the same token, the modernization and development of the Tibetan plateau via an influx of Chinese merchants, managers, and technicans, etc., combined with discriminatory policies, can only have the effect of making large segments of the Tibetan population marginal to their homeland, economically and in other ways.

That the Chinese government is encouraging migration into Tibet cannot be questioned. Prior to the 1980s, before the government began actively using incentives to stimulate economic and social activity, most of the Chinese in Tibet were, by all accounts, workers and officials who were highly unenthusiastic about their forced postings to Tibet. Many found the region's altitude, local culture, and material conditions to be severe hardships for which they

44

received no real recompense. This has changed drastically during the last four or five years. A new breed of Chinese settler has arrived in Tibet. The new settlers are not forced to go to Tibet; by and large they come because they know that under the central government's market oriented reforms there is a profit to be made in Tibet. The authorities see the tourist industry as one of the main instruments for the economic development of Tibet.* In the TAR, that industry is producing enough of an economic boom not only to draw Chinese from outside the region to work in it, but to spawn other economic possibilities that draw more Chinese. In addition to Chinese shopkeepers, hotel workers and restaurateurs, all sorts of other Chinese entrepreneurs and itinerant traders are coming into Tibet as well. These new settlers are changing the economic picture in Tibet as a strong and growing tourist trade generates money in Lhasa and a few other places.

The campaign to encourage Chinese settlers to move to Tibet includes appeals to various sentiments, including the romantic (something reminiscent of earlier Chinese encouragement of migration to Xinjiang, and even earlier Soviet migration into Central Asia). One recent work published in Chinese in Lhasa tells prospective newcomers: "Whether you come to do pioneering work or to open things up, no matter how much you discover, you will discover what is most valuable to you: you will discover yourself."**

Areas of Discrimination Against the Tibetan Population

One area of clear-cut inequality between Tibetans and Chinese, obvious even to many casual visitors to the TAR, is in housing. In most of the urban areas of Tibet one notices new dwelling quarters being put up very quickly. By and large the Tibetan quarters of most towns and cities are surrounded and

---

*   For some of the reasoning behind this see Gu Xiaorong and Hu Zuyuan, "Lun liuyouye zai Xizang jingji zhong de zhanlue diwei," Xizang yenjiu, 1986.2, pp. 16-19 and 31; and Xia Xueying, "Chongfen fahui ziyuan youshi, jiakuai fazhan Xizang liuyouye," Xizang jingji tan-suo, 1986.1, pp. 25-26 and 18. Other articles in publications from Tibet take up a similar theme.

**   Ma Lihua, Zhui ni dao gaoyuan (Lhasa, 1986), p. 9.

often dwarfed by larger and more expansive new Chinese quarters. In a good many cases, these new buildings are equipped with running water as well as electricity. The Tibetan quarters of such towns remain without running water and in many cases without reasonable sanitation facilities. The buildings are not well kept up, nor are they renovated or restored. For the most part, they are being allowed to decay. The Tibetan quarters of larger towns usually have electricity. It is only on at certain times of the day, however, and it has fulfilled a function for the authorities as much as for the Tibetans. In the past, it has allowed the authorities to pipe political statements and commentary into the streets during the day and evening.

It is in the urban areas that Chinese migrants live, and it is largely there that electricity is available. The lesser villages that are found scattered in various reaches of the plateau are electrified only if they lie along a major highway. Thus, the greater part of Tibet remains untouched by development, its population seemingly considered significant only to the extent that Chinese migrants appear in their midst. As one Tibetan put it:

> Villages far away, away from main roads, have no electricity. But its not just far away villages. For example in the southern part of the [Tibetan] Autonomous Region the road is only good to the airport....[A road is good] if it's a military route.... If it is only for [Tibetan] people no consideration is given to making a road....Electricity goes to the prefecture and county seats where Chinese are. Tibetans [elsewhere] have no electricity.

Certain circumstances of life in Tibet force one to conclude that the new and extensive housing is almost exclusively for Chinese who have moved to Tibet. That is also the contention of Tibetans in Tibet, who note also that most of the migrants are from the neighboring (and very populous) province of Sichuan. Others come from Gansu and regions further to the east.

Tibetans are generally made to maintain their residence in one place. While travel and pilgrimage are permitted, and while this has allowed Tibetans inside and outside the TAR to visit Lhasa and other areas of religious significance, they are only rarely allowed to move to a city such as Lhasa and to take part in its growing commercial life. There appears to be a clearly defined policy to restrict Tibetans from taking a large part in the economic changes that are occurring in Tibet. In that sense, the economic integration of Tibet into the rest of the PRC is taking place through the marginalization of Tibetan economic life. Thus, obvious efforts are made to accommodate Chinese migrants to the plateau. For Tibetans, the story is quite different. According to Tibetans in Tibet, should a Tibetan from A-mdo or Khams come to Lhasa on pilgrimage, and desire to stay there and try his or her hand at the economic possibilities presented by the new policies, it is almost certain that the local authorities will force the person to leave. The situation was described by Tibetans in Tibet as follows. One informed observer noted:

> They [the Chinese] all have papers allowing them to come to Lhasa. Whether they need or don't need passes to reside in Lhasa, that I don't know....but they get places immediately. We Tibetans....can't afford to put up places....All the new buildings going up are for Chinese residents. Tibetans don't live in them. Its easy for the Chinese to stay in Lhasa....If you're a Tibetan from A-mdo or Khams it isn't easy. When you get to Lhasa you need not register for seven days. After seven days you have to register with the PSB and get a pass. By staying with relatives you can get a pass for one or two months....Near the Post Office are pilgrims who come to Lhasa and who live in tents. They stay for a couple of days and then go back. They don't stay in [homes in] Lhasa. If they stay in a house they have to register. The Chinese know just how many Tibetans from A-mdo and Khams there are in Lhasa....But for Chinese to come, put up buildings....that's all extremely easy.

> According to another Tibetan whom we regard as credible:

> We can't say what the total population of greater Lhasa is; it's treated as a secret. But the greater part of the population is Chinese....The Chinese are now in the Barkor [Bar-skor; the road encircling the Jokhang, it draws pilgrims and is the main commercial area of the Tibetan quarter]. This is a new thing....
> The Chinese government says it withdraws most Chinese from Tibet. But for every Chinese that goes five more come....They live in the areas below the Potala, below Drepung, below Sera....There are many Chinese merchants now. They come from all over China, from Sichuan, Gansu, Zhejiang....As for

these merchants, as Chinese they have "back door" relations [with the authorities] and therefore they get places....Taking shops as an example, a Tibetan who lives here can't get a decent place. The Chinese, because they have connections with each other, get shops and get places to live....If you come from A-mdo or Khams you can't get a place to stay. They [the authorities] will tell you that you don't have a registration pass from this area. You are not a resident of this area. When Tibetans from A-mdo, and Nag-chu....come to Lhasa thinking they would like to live here they are not allowed to remain. They are not allowed to have a place to stay....

A story that appeared in the Tibetan exile press accords with the description of the situation presented by Tibetans in the TAR. It told the story of some Tibetans from Lho-kha, the southern portion of Central Tibet, who had left their home region because of a critical situation that had arisen in spring agricultural work some months ago. Arriving in Lhasa and intending to do construction work, they put up tents in which to live. Shortly thereafter PSB officials arrived to check their papers. When they could produce no residence permits for Lhasa, the officials ordered them to leave. They protested that they had more of a right to live in Lhasa than the Chinese construction workers in the city, but the officials refused to allow them to stay. They were put onto trucks and sent back to Lho-kha.*

The impression one gets is of a studied discrimination designed to integrate Tibet as much as possible into the economy of the PRC by emphasizing and giving special consideration to the role of Chinese in the region's economic development. As such, much of what one reads about the development of Tibet is concerned more with the region than with its people. This is not to say that no benefits whatever accrue to Tibetans as a result of the improving economic picture in the TAR. Tibetans, however, are not the primary beneficiaries of this changed situation. Overall, they remain among the poorest people in the PRC. Of course a certain degree of the economic growth in Tibet must inevitably

---

*   "Bod-mir rang-gi yul-du 'gro-sdod-kyi rang-dbang rtsa-ba-nas med-pa," Shes-bya, September, 1987, p. 19.

48

reach the Tibetans. Moreover, policies implemented in the Tibetan countryside, such as the tax moratorium on agricultural and pastoral production introduced in 1984, have greatly improved the picture there in comparison to what it was only five or six years ago. But Tibetans are really not central to the major economic development going on in the TAR. More and more it is a Chinese economy that is sprouting in the urban areas of Tibet, and Tibetans are marginal to it. Today, conveniences in the TAR depend largely on its Chinese technicians, managers, entrepreneurs, and tourist industry workers. Without the latter, electrical power, transportation, and other important elements in the Tibetan infrastructure would suffer drastically. Chinese are purposefully being made an essential part of the new economic picture in Tibet.

* * *

Part of the reason for the increasingly central role of Chinese in the infrastructure of the TAR, and of almost all other Tibetan areas, lies in the differences between the education that Tibetans and Chinese receive. The influx of large numbers of Chinese into Tibet plays a role in this inequality. It has required the creation of a Chinese-language educational curriculum in the school system, largely for the newcomers, and very much superior to the Tibetan-language curriculum.

By all accounts, the school system in Tibet prior to the early 1980s was a shambles. It has subsequently undergone major changes, however, and is vastly different from what it was only six or seven years ago (although in the eastern portions of Tibet, outside the TAR, schooling is still very poor). One feature of the new system that Tibetans in Tibet have made note of is the increased emphasis on Tibetan as the language for elementary schools in certain parts of the TAR. This is largely in accord with the 1984 Law on Regional Autonomy for Minority Nationalities. Article 37 of this law states that in schools in which students of a given minority nationality predominate, their written and spoken language should be used if conditions permit. The implication is that this refers to elementary education; the same article states that in the upper levels of elemen-

49

tary school or in middle schools a Chinese-language curriculum should be instituted "to spread the common language used by the entire nation."*

In actual practice in Tibet, a Tibetan-language education is largely limited to elementary schools. Although the situation has improved over what it was several years ago, education in the TAR is still not universal, and after elementary school there is often no choice as to whether one will follow a Tibetan or Chinese curriculum. Schools with only the latter predominate. In those instances where choice is possible, it is only the Chinese curriculum that can impart a semblance of modern education. Little or no effort has been made to provide qualified teachers and textbooks so that a reasonable level of post-elementary school instruction may be given in Tibetan in the TAR. The situation both inside and outside the TAR has been described to Asia Watch as follows:**

> Most Tibetan students in school study in Chinese, although recently education in Tibetan has been strengthened....In all bureaus and posts you have to use Chinese; Tibetan is not used in any positions. Nominally, to make a display for the outside, to pretty things up, [the authorities publicly] talk about how Tibetan must be used....In reality no bureaus or posts use Tibetan [as a normal working language]....In the Lhasa schools Chinese make up the majority....All over the place the Chinese have set up schools for themselves....They don't study Tibetan, but Tibetans are made to study Chinese. In elementary schools Tibetans study Tibetan and Chinese. In middle schools students study Tibetan and Chinese....In institutions of higher learning one studies science...but Tibetans....don't study science. There are no Tibetan-language textbooks for this; they're all in Chinese. In the bookstores....the greater part of the books are in Chinese. Science ... is in Chinese. Only a minimal amount is in Tibetan.

> Our schools [in the east] are at a make-do level...In these elementary schools students learn both Tibetan and Chinese;

---

* Zhonghua renmin gongheguo minzu quyu zizhifa (Lhasa, n.d. [1984?]), p. 13.

** Each paragraph represents a different Tibetan source; we regard each as credible.

this is all over....In middle schools [it is felt that] Tibetan serves no purpose, so they are for the greater part Chinese-language [institutions]. If you don't know Chinese you can't take an examination to get into a college. The general level of Tibetan [in terms of reading and writing] is practically nonexistent....[Tibetan education] is a fraud in the east, really. The teachers who teach Tibetan have no degree of culture themselves....

[In 1986, in Lhasa's No. 1 Middle School] out of 28 classes 12 were for Tibetans....Out of 1451 students 933 were Tibetan and 518 were Chinese. Not only were the Chinese students not learning Tibetan, 387 of the Tibetan students were not learning Tibetan either. Only 546 Tibetans were learning Tibetan. Only 7 of the schools 111 teachers taught Tibetan....Only 30 teachers were Tibetan. They say the best teachers teach classes for Chinese students, the worst teachers teach classes for Tibetan students.

The current primacy of the Chinese language within the educational system of Tibet has been acknowledged recently by Chinese authorities who note that "[e]xcept for the Tibetan language classes, all courses are taught mainly in Chinese in middle and high schools [in the TAR]."* At the college level too, Chinese students and the Chinese language have primacy. Tibetans maintain that in 1984 the total number of students at institutions of higher education in the TAR totalled 2,474, out of which Tibetans were only slightly more than twenty-five percent. The following year, when the Tibetan Normal College was remade into the University of Tibet, its seven academic departments included only two in which the Tibetan language was used: the Department of Tibetan Language and Literature and the Department of Tibetan Medicine.

There is no question that the language issue with respect to education is a complicated one. Nonetheless, one sees in the combination of Chinese policies the penalization of Tibetans on the basis of their mother tongue. Within the educational system of their own regions, they are at a disadvantage vis-a-vis

---

* "Culture, Education and Health Care: A Dialogue on Tibet (V)," Beijing Review, December 7-13, 1987, p. 24.

Chinese migrants and their children, who do not have to master a new language in order to get something of a modern education. The inequalities inherent in this system are manifested most clearly when jobs and employment are at issue. The practical result is to place Tibetans at the bottom rung of society in most urban areas, making them effectively marginal to the development of Tibet and to the region's future.

* * *

The question of employment is closely connected with that of education, for it is the educational qualifications of many in the Tibetan population that keeps them peripheral. According to Tibetans in Tibet, decent positions in bureaus or elsewhere in the infrastructure of the TAR and adjacent Tibetan regions require a high level of Chinese, both in reading and writing. Such positions as exist are accessible via examinations that are given solely in Chinese. It is said that even Tibetans who have reasonably good levels of Chinese are still no match for migrants or their children for whom Chinese is a first language (and who in almost all cases know no Tibetan). The result of such conditions has been an acute unemployment problem among Tibetans, including those with a middle school education. There are important exceptions to this pattern, but nevertheless, a large number of Tibetans in urban areas are unemployed except for whatever day work they can find. This sort of work is often manual construction labor, but even that doesn't provide enough jobs. Unemployment in the urban areas of the plateau is said to remain a critical problem. Reportedly, the local government in the TAR has turned its attention to the situation, but little has yet been done to ameliorate it. According to many Tibetans, the most technically advanced position a Tibetan seems to find is as a truck driver. That in itself demonstrates the link between the lack of scientific and technical education in Tibetan and the subsequent employment prospects for Tibetans.

The situation in Tibetan areas outside the TAR is, if anything, worse. Unemployed young people are seen commonly in the towns. Many travellers have taken note of the seemingly related problem of alcoholism, both inside and outside the TAR, though Tibetans in Tibet now say that problem has diminished.* Nevertheless, the problem of employment in the eastern portion of the Tibetan Plateau is said to be particularly serious. According to one report from Tibet that we believe to be credible:

> In Khams and A-mdo Tibetans coming out of county-level schools who get jobs are very few. Out of 100, except for maybe one, two or three, none will get... posts as "cadres"** of any sort...so [the others] go back to their families. You have to know Chinese in order to get work. Tibetan is useless. In a Chinese office, only Chinese is of use....There are so many people in the east without work.

The preeminent position of the Chinese language throughout the Tibetan Plateau has produced a situation in which Tibetans are at a strong disadvantage in finding positions. Tibetans perceive an inherent bias in this that favors Chinese migrants and their children.

Aside from the question of cadre positions, Tibetans also say they are at a disadvantage in commerce when faced with the new influx of Chinese who are coming to Tibet as entrepreneurs. One Tibetan shopkeeper noted:

> To start a shop...one has to go to the trade supervision office... and then to the tax office. There one pays money and then gets a permit. We are not treated as Chinese are. We must first go to our own district supervisory committees and get an introduction....Then we go to [the other offices] to get the permit. The Chinese arrive with introductions from their own areas and immediately get a permit....The money for the permit is the same for all....but there is bribery [involved in the process], and here the Chinese have the connections.

By and large, Tibetans state that the taxes and other fees they have to pay as merchants are not any greater than those that Chinese merchants pay. They maintain that they face discrimination in other ways; that the Chinese have

---

* Interestingly, they say this is due to remarks on the subject made by the Dalai Lama to Tibetans visiting in India.

** In Tibetan, las-byed-pa. Tibetans generally use this term to refer not simply to government or party workers per se, but to any who have a position, generally involving some skill, training or education, and an affiliation with any sector of the large state bureaucracy.

no trouble getting started in business while they themselves lack the "back door" connections. In any event, the continuing proliferation of Chinese entrepreneurial businesses is something that one cannot avoid noticing in Tibet. It is reasonably safe to say that most such businesses are in Chinese hands, in spite of steep taxes that confront anyone venturing to do business in the marketplace (and to some degree offset the tax moratorium in the Tibetan countryside).

* * *

There is another area in which inequalities related to the influx of Chinese may be seen, although this is perhaps not so obvious at first: family planning. As is by now well known, Chinese families are enjoined from having more than one child each. At the same time, a degree of publicity has been given to the fact that Tibetans (and other minority nationalities) are exempt from this policy.* Lately, however, public statements in this regard have been modified. Now it is officially said by PRC spokesmen that:

> We only encourage Tibetan cadres and state-owned enterprise employees to practice family planning. Under this policy they are encouraged to have one child and permitted to have two. Special cases may have three children. These policies have never been applied to Tibetan herdsmen and farmers.**

Unfortunately Tibetans in Tibet maintain that this is not at all the case. According to them, the two child limit is applied universally in the TAR and in neighboring Tibetan regions. Tibetans who spoke to us on this question were unequivocal in their remarks. From their descriptions, the methods used to enforce the limit seem fairly similar to those used elsewhere in the PRC with regard to the one child per family limit. These include financial and other pressures.

---

* "Tibetans Healthier, Better Educated," Beijing Review, October 15, 1984, p. 11; "China's policy of 'one couple one child' does not apply to Tibet where more population has been encouraged as the economy develops."

** "Religion, Crime and Citizens' Rights: A Dialogue on Tibet (II)," Beijing Review, October 26-November 1, 1987, p. 26.

Tibetans maintain, moreover, that abortions carried out without the consent — or even the knowledge — of the mother are by no means unknown. Asia Watch has been told that:

> Tibetans are not allowed to have more than two children. Third or fourth children will not be able to get ration cards or registration cards. This is all over Tibet....A pregnant woman, prior to the birth of a [third] child is given a medicine to induce an abortion. Things are done in this way. One doesn't have the freedom to abort or not. If a woman is in a hospital and in the course of an examination [it is seen that she is pregnant], the child is aborted. She is given medicine and an abortion is done without her even being asked. If a woman still wants to have a [third] child she can be given such medicine in the course of an examination for an illness. She doesn't know what the medicine is for....This was done to people whom I know personally.

It is said that abortions performed on Tibetan women without their consent are done frequently at the hospital in Xining, the capital of Qinghai province. That portion of the plateau is subject to the same two child limit as the TAR. As in the TAR, a third child will not get ration or registration cards. There is a fine of RMB 300 for having a third child.

Asia Watch is aware of the seriousness of reports with respect to involuntary abortion. However, the information available to us suggests that these abuses do occur in Tibet. Asia Watch does not question the right of nations to adopt family planning policies. However, abortions performed or induced *without* a mother's consent violate a woman's privacy in a most brutal way. We do not know how widespread this practice may be, but we remain concerned about it.

Questions of discrimination and the influx of Chinese into Tibet intersect when one realizes that only a few years ago the government of the PRC was contending that family size restrictions would not apply to Tibet in order to build up the population and thus develop Tibet's economy.* With such restrictions

---

* "Tibetans Healthier, Better Educated," Beijing Review, October 15, 1984, p. 11.

now being imposed, and with Chinese migration being encouraged at the same time, it is evident that policy has shifted from one in which the Tibetans were to play a large economic role in the TAR and on the plateau, to one in which that central role is consciously being given to Chinese. While a policy of two children per family would have the effect of keeping the Tibetan population stable under only the most ideal of conditions, the plateau's Chinese population is continuing to grow, as a result of officially encouraged migration. Accordingly we conclude that Tibetans are increasingly being moved by design into disadvantageous economic and social positions vis-a-vis the plateau's growing Chinese population in the cities and towns to which the Chinese are drawn.

THE AUTUMN 1987 DEMONSTRATIONS

The issue of Tibet and of human rights in Tibet was brought sharply into public view this past fall as a result of a series of three demonstrations held in Lhasa to which the Chinese authorities responded with violent repression. Press reports and eye-witness accounts of what happened in Lhasa have been clear in describing the events of September 27, October 1, and October 6 as nonviolent in origin; violence having erupted on October 1 only when Chinese PSB officials beat and fired on unarmed Tibetan demonstrators. The aftermath of these demonstrations has been a wave of arrests, an interdiction on travel to Lhasa (except for short term, lucrative tour groups — who are always lodged in the Lhasa Hotel, far from the Tibetan quarter), and vociferous denunciations by the Chinese authorities of any criticism of its Tibetan policies. Tibetan exile sources have reported anti-Chinese demonstrations in other Tibetan cities during and after the unrest in Lhasa but it has not been possible to verify these reports. Neither has it been possible to research the cases of those arrested during these events, as was done for several other Tibetan prisoners in an earlier section of this report.

It is the position of Asia Watch that the arrests, beatings, and deaths that followed the demonstrations must be seen against a pattern of violent repression aimed at sentiment and opinion at variance with the official line on Tibet. While this report on the human rights situation in Tibet is concerned for the most part only with the record of the present (i.e., post-1980) Chinese government, it is fair to say that the PRC has shown a disregard for some of the most basic norms of human rights for the greater part of its rule in Tibet.

Asia Watch cannot stress too strongly its belief that China's actions in Tibet in the fall of 1987 (condemned in most quarters) follow from and accord with its previous record on human rights in Tibet. Freedom of speech and assembly, protections against torture, and public trials: all go by the wayside where dissent on basic PRC policies in Tibet is involved. If anything, the Chinese response was atypical only by virtue of the shock and chagrin that the authorities appear to have felt at the very public and unambiguous nature of the demonstrations. Otherwise, much that characterizes the official response to the recent demonstrations also characterizes the treatment of dissent in Tibet over the last several years.

A number of reports dealing with the protests of September 27, October 1, and October 6, and the actions taken by the authorities in their wake have reached Asia Watch. We believe that there is enough material now available to allow us to venture a short summary description of these events.*

September 27: In the morning a group of 20-30 monks from Drepung marched around the Jokhang carrying home-made Tibetan flags (possession of which is illegal) and shouting Tibetan independence slogans. They were joined by approximately 150-200 others who then began marching down People's Road, from the Jokhang to the seat of the TAR administration. Just before reaching the government compound the monks, along with a few of the other demonstrators, were arrested by police. Witnesses report that the arrests were accompanied by beatings. The behavior of the demonstrators was wholly nonviolent.

October 1: Another demonstration began in the morning. Led by more than 20 monks from Sera monastery, approximately 300 people made three circuits around the Jokhang shouting Tibetan independence slogans. 50-60 were beaten and arrested and taken into the PSB bureau. A crowd estimated at 2,000-3,000 gathered in front of the PSB building facing the front of the Jokhang and demanded the release of those arrested. Soon the Chinese brought cameras and began photographing people in the crowd, an act that was seen by those gathered there as preparatory to later arrests. Chinese with cameras were

---

* We may also note that these events received widespread coverage in the world media. There is little need here to cite specific journalistic reports, except in certain instances. One may look in any of the leading newspapers or news magazines during the period of the demonstrations to find coverage. The most detailed reconstructions of the events described below comes from the observations of a number of tourists, who pooled their information into one report: "Western Account of Lhasa Demonstrations," Tibetan Review, November, 1987, pp. 5-8. An 11-page telex from Kathmandu containing the report of two Westerners who acted as translators for the other tourists (particularly for Dr. Blake Kerr, an American doctor who treated many who were wounded during the October 1 demonstration) has been made available to Asia Watch, and contains much important information.

stoned and driven away. The crowd then tried to break into the PSB bureau and free those arrested. PSB vehicles in front of the station were smashed and set on fire. The station door was set on fire in order to allow the crowd to break in and free those arrested. Armed police who arrived with fire fighters were turned back by stone throwers. Shortly thereafter the first shots were fired by PSB forces from elsewhere in the vicinity. Following this, more people arrived including young monks from Sera. Some of these monks began running into the burning PSB bureau and, in the resulting confusion, most of the prisoners are believed to have escaped. By this time, the firing by the PSB forces from nearby roofs became obvious to people below. Fatalities followed as the police began firing into the crowd. Finally, additional PSB forces arrived and began firing in order to clear people away from the front of the burning PSB station. One group of Tibetans picked up the body of a 16-year-old boy who was killed and carried it through the streets shouting angry slogans. The police continued to shoot sporadically from roofs and from positions in the square in front of the Jokhang.

Many of the cameras used by Chinese photographers were grabbed and smashed by people in the crowd. The police arrested and later released several Westerners after taking the film from their cameras.* Reportedly, these rolls of film were used in order to identify Tibetans who participated in the unrest. Throughout the rest of the day and into the next morning Tibetans looted files and papers from the burnt police station. Observers believe that up to 13 Tibetans died during the disturbances, while another 13 were seriously injured. Almost all of these had been shot. Observers are unanimous in stating that no Tibetans were seen with guns. A Chinese spokesman later claimed that the Tibetans had grabbed guns away from the PSB forces.**

---

*   A particularly graphic report, with photographs of the procession carrying the body of the 16-year-old boy who was killed, was written by two French journalists who were detained at this time: Christine de Colombel and Sophie Ristelhueber, "Le jeudi rouge de Lhassa," Le Nouvel Observateur, October 30-November 5, 1987.

**   "Tibetan Protest for Independence Becomes Violent," The New York Times, October 3, 1987.

October 6: A group of approximately 100 Tibetans formed ranks at Drepung monastery and began marching down toward the TAR administrative compound in Lhasa. When they reached the compound, about 60 were arrested and put on trucks by soldiers carrying rifles with fixed bayonets.

* * *

Following these events, severely repressive measures were taken by the authorities. Military reinforcements were flown to Tibet, troops were paraded in Lhasa in a show of force aimed at the Tibetan population, and PSB units took up positions at the main monasteries in the Lhasa region.* Just as ominously, individual tourists, i.e., those not in tour groups who generally stay at one of the small hotels in the old Tibetan quarter, were ordered out of Tibet as were foreign journalists. The latter move was made on the rather specious grounds that none of the journalists' visits had been arranged and approved according to government regulations, even though local TAR officials had been dealing with them up to that point in official capacities.** At this writing, the ban on individual travellers and journalists is still in effect. The gravity of the situation is reflected in the comments of one Westerner in Tibet who was told by Tibetans that but for the presence of Westerners in Lhasa on October 1, there would surely have been a massacre in front of the PSB post. Weeks after the demonstrations, Lhasa remained tense. Chinese patrols reportedly continued to sweep through the streets, while nighttime raids on individual homes to check identification and residence documents were carried out in the Tibetan quarter.*** Leniency was promised to participants in the demonstrations who turned themselves in to the authorities by October 15th. Asia Watch has little information on the results of this offer. It is clear, though, that distrust of the

---

*   "Authorities Stage 'Show of Force' in Lhasa," FBIS-CHI-87-195, October 8, 1987, pp. 21-22, quoting an Agence France-Presse dispatch of the same day.

**   See "Reporters Ordered to Leave," FBIS-CHI-87-195, October 8, 1987, p. 23, quoting a Xinhua dispatch of the same day; and "AFP Report," FBIS-CHI-87-195, October 8, 1987, pp. 23-24, quoting an Agence France-Presse dispatch of the same day.

***   "Police Reported to Patrol Lhasa Streets," FBIS-CHI-87-226, November 24, 1987, p. 38, quoting an Agence France-Presse dispatch of the same day.

Chinese authorities was common in Lhasa; many of the wounded preferred to be treated by Westerners rather than to risk going to the Chinese hospitals and being arrested on the spot.

* * *

Asia Watch has been informed that at least 300-400 people were arrested in Lhasa after the demonstrations. The number may be ultimately far higher, however. It is reported that police raids in the Tibetan quarters appeared to increase after October 15th, when the offer of leniency expired. Tibetans also believe that at least 19 people died in police custody as a result of injuries sustained after arrest. At this writing, it is difficult to get precise information about what is happening in Tibet, in large part due to the expulsion from Tibet of Western journalists and individual travellers. Organized tour groups are allowed in, but these are easily controlled and monitered, as they all stay at the Lhasa Hotel, far enough away from the Tibetan quarter to pose no problems for the authorities.

Asia Watch is very concerned about the steps taken by the authorities in Lhasa in the aftermath of the demonstrations. The fact that the authorities felt it necessary to expel the foreign press only leads us to believe that the secrecy which serves as an important element in political repression and human rights abuses in the TAR is spreading further.

In the period shortly after the demonstrations, Asia Watch received reports from Westerners and Tibetan exile sources concerning political arrests and treatment in prison — including torture, and even reports of deaths — and other measures that must be taken seriously in light of what we believe to be a pattern of human rights abuses in Tibet.

* * *

Two Westerners who translated and helped coordinate medical assistance for wounded Tibetans compiled an 11-page report. We draw on that report for the information in the paragraphs that follow.

The monks arrested on September 27 were: Jampey Changchub ('Jam-dpal byang-chub), 26; Jampey Lezang ('Jam-dpal legs-bzang), 26; Ngawang Gyaltsen (Ngag-dbang rgyal-mtshan), 25; Ngawang Khetsun (Ngag-dbang mkhas-btsun), 23; Ngawang Pulbung (Ngag-dbang phul-byung), 26; Ngawang Penbar (Ngag-dbang dpal-'bar), 22; Ngawang Tsognyi (Ngag-dbang tshogs-gnyis), 24; Ngawang Obar (Ngag-dbang 'od-'bar), 22; Ngawang Rinchen (Ngag-dbang rin-chen), 24; Ngawang Tashi (Ngag-dbang bkra-shis), 23; Ngawang Tardo (Ngag-dbang thar-'dod), 21; Jampey Tseten ('Jam-dpal tshe-brtan), 23; Jampey Tsering ('Jam-dpal tshe-ring), 20; Dorjee Trinley (Rdo-rje 'phrin-las), 24; Ngawang Chodra (Ngag-dbang chos-grags), 21; Ngawang Osel (Ngag-dbang 'od-gsal), 19; Jampey Nyima ('Jam-dpal nyi-ma), 23; Jampey Monlam ('Jam-dpal smon-lam), 24; Jampey Losel ('Jam-dpal blo-gsal), 25; Ngawang Domsung (Ngag-dbang sdom-srung), 23; and Ngawang Pelzang (Ngag-dbang dpal-bzang), 27.*

The first seven are from the Tolungdechen (Stod-lung Bde-chen) area, the next five from Phenpo ('Phan-po), and the remaining nine from the Drigung ('Bri gung) and Taktse Lho-kha (Stag-rtse Lho-kha) areas. Nine of them are said to have been released on or about October 27th.**

On October 1st, 50-60 people were beaten and arrested by PSB forces in the morning after marching around the Jokhang. The group included 23 monks from Sera, 3 from Nechung, and 8 from the Jokhang. In the afternoon 20 people were arrested in the Barkor, beaten with rifle butts and rocks, and then released. Two of these were treated by Westerners. Five foreigners were arrested briefly and had their camera film confiscated.

Three of the monks who were arrested and had then managed to escape from the burning PSB building that day were recaptured by the PSB. Their names are given as: Kesang Donyo (Skal-bzang don-yod), 35; Jampey Senge

---

*   Nb. the transcriptions (preceding parenthetical transliteration) of the names are given as they are in the original telex report.

**   "Xizang Deals Leniently with 13 Rioters," FBIS-CHI-87-209, October 29, 1987, p. 44, quoting a Radio Lhasa broadcast of October 28, 1987. The nine monks who were released were: Ngawang Chodra, Ngawang Pelzang, Ngawang Penbar, Ngawang Domsung, Ngawang Tashi, Jempey Lezang, Jampey Tseten, Jampey Nyima, and another whose name is difficult to decipher from the transcription, but who is probably Ngawang Pulbung or, more properly, Ngawang Puljung.

('Jam-dpal seng-ge), 36; and Tashi Tsering (Bkra-shis tshe-ring), also known as Gyaltsen Thar chin (Rgyal-mtshan mthar-phyin), 20.

That night the PSB raided Sera in a search for other escaped monks. During the raid, some monks were hit with rifle butts. The following were arrested: Kesang tsering (Skal-bzang tshe-ring), 31; Dawa Tsering (Zla-ba tshe-ring), 27; Phuntsok Dondhup (Phun-tshogs don-grub), 27; Jampey ('Jam-dpal), 27; and Lobsang Sherab (Blo-bzang shes-rab), 22. Another monk, Gelong Lobsang Kungga (Dge-slong Blo-bzang kun-dga'), 26, was believed to have been arrested or in hiding.

Arrests during the next few days are said to have swept up at least 300 people; some say 600 is more likely, and others say that the number goes into the thousands. There was a good deal of brutality involved in the arrests. Those arrested on October 6 were walking peacefully to the TAR administrative compound. In front of a crowd that included Westerners, they were arrested and severely beaten with rifle butts, sticks, leather belts, and rocks, generally after they had been shackled. A few days later, some of the monks were released and examined by a Western doctor who found a number to have severe wounds that had received only rudimentary attention.

On October 26 or 27 two more monks were arrested at Sera: Lobsang Dawa (Blo-bzang zla-ba), about 24; and Thubten Tsering (Thub-bstan tshe-ring), 21.

Indirect information received by Westerners in Lhasa at the time paints a poor image of the conditions under which these people are imprisoned. These conditions accord with those that have been described elsewhere in this report. The prisoners were beaten, often severely. It is said that one woman had her back broken and received no medical treatment. The PSB officials used iron rods and cattle prods on prisoners, applying shocks for up to five minutes, according to Tibetans who had access to information on the situation in the prisons. The daily ration in prison for these new political prisoners was two plain momo and water. Many prisoners seem to be held in solitary confinement. Parcels could not be sent into them, nor (with only one known exception) could they have visitors.

Outside of prison, the authorities are said to have organized criticism meetings in monasteries and other units at which participants were required to denounce the demonstrators, Tibetan independence, and the Dalai Lama. This tactic was not always successful. It is reported that after October 20, denunciations of the Dalai Lama were no longer demanded.

* * *

Tibetan exile sources have supplied the names and approximate ages (if known) of the following twelve Lhasa residents who are also believed to be under arrest as a result of the repression following the demonstrations: Dorjee Dolma (Rdo-rje sgrol-ma), 30; Tseten Dolkar (Tshe-brtan sgrol-dkar), 30; Tenzin (Bstan-'dzin), 22; Migmar (Mig-dmar), 30; Yeshi Yangchen (Ye-shes dbyangs-can), 32; Thinlay ('Phrin-las), 40; Jampa Ngodup (Byams-pa dngos-grub), 38; Nyima Tsamchoe (Nyi-ma mtshams-gcod), 19; Chungdak (Chung-bdag); Kalden (Skal-ldan); Dekhi (Bde-skyid), 28; and Tseten Dorjee (Tshe-brtan rdo-rje), 20.

For its part, China has recently reported the release and pardon of 59 participants in the September and October clashes on the grounds that they had recognized the error of their actions. The names of the 59 were not given and the report maintained that only 10 or so people were still under investigation for involvement in the incidents.* At the same time, it has been reported that an Austrian student, Felix Haller, is being held under house arrest in Lhasa for supporting Tibetan independence demonstrations. The same report states that as recently as December 19, twenty Tibetan nuns had carried out such a demonstration near the Jokhang. The report also mentions a demonstration by monks in Ganden against the Chinese PSB presence at the monastery. Eighty were said to have been arrested, most of whom were subsequently released.**

---

*   "Lasashi zhengfa bumen xuanbu jueding kuanda chuli yipi canjia saoluanzhe," Renmin ribao, January 22, 1988.

**   "Austrian Student Under House Arrest," FBIS-CHI-88-003, January 6, 1988, pp. 6-7, quoting an Agence France-Presse dispatch of January 5, 1988.

CHINA'S POSITION ON THE HUMAN RIGHTS SITUATION IN TIBET

The reaction of PRC officials to the upsurge in critical concern about Tibet has been angry and vociferous, not least because of continuing sensitivity about various facets of the Tibetan issue in general that seem to resurface continually. The government of the PRC, and those who speak for it officially, maintain that there is no human rights problem in Tibet and that any who say there is are perhaps simply seeking the restoration of "feudal serfdom." The recent disturbances, they say, are simply the work of a "handful of splittists." Beyond this, China's position with regard to all aspects of the Tibetan issue is that no external involvement or interest is to be tolerated. Foreign debate and concern on the subject, particularly when other governments or their officials are involved, have been roundly denounced by the PRC as interference in China's internal affairs.

China's rigid position on one aspect of the human rights issue as it related to Tibet was made clear in Spring 1987 after an opinion piece in the *Washington Post* had focused attention on the question of political imprisonment and mistreatment of prisoners in Tibet.* Responding to questions touched off by the article and raised by foreign reporters at a press conference in Beijing, the Panchen Lama spoke on behalf of the government. His remarks were quoted in a Chinese press report:

> "This sort of talk is utterly baseless." He said "I can inform everybody that there are no political prisoners in Tibet's prisons. There is only a very small number of criminals who have seriously violated public and social order, such as thieves and murderers. The government punishes them according to

---

*   John F. Avedon, "The Rape of Tibet," _The Washington Post_, March 29, 1987.

65

law." The Panchen Lama said that the government treats these prisoners humanely and has no need for corporal punishment.*

A number of other developments in 1987 also elicited comment on the human rights situation in Tibet from Chinese spokesmen. On June 18, the U.S. House of Representatives passed an amendment to the Foreign Relations Authorization Act that contained sharp criticism of China's practices. From September 18 through September 29, the Dalai Lama was in the United States and he met in Washington D.C. with members of the House of Representatives Human Rights Caucus, and raised the Tibetan issue with them. On October 6, in the wake of the attention which the Lhasa demonstrations drew to the Tibetan issue, the U.S. Senate passed, 98-0, a motion to condemn Chinese actions in the region. On October 14, two Foreign Affairs subcommittees of the U.S. House of Representatives held a joint hearing on the question of human rights in Tibet, while on the same day the issue was raised in the European Parliament and the German Bundestag. Shortly afterwards, a request by a U.S. Congressional group to send a delegation to Tibet was rejected by the Chinese government.

The Chinese reaction has been almost uniformly unyielding. The government of the PRC maintains that there is no human rights problem in Tibet. As already noted, the Chinese authorities have only acknowledged that they hold 28 "counterrevolutionary" prisoners. Even here, however, there is a problem with regard to what the Chinese authorities consider a political crime. In an official (and rare) statement on the case of Geshe Lobsang Wangchuk — undoubtedly the most well-known Tibetan political prisoner — a spokesman objected to his being described as a "criminal of conscience" (*sic,* i.e., a prisoner of conscience). According to the statement, "there is no 'crime of conscience' in our Criminal Law, and therefore 'criminal of conscience' is nonexistent."**

Similarly, Chinese officials have made it clear that those who participated in the September and October demonstrations, or who nonviolently

---

*   "Banchan xiang Zhongwai jizhe jieshao yuan Zang jijinhui," Renmin ribao, April 17, 1987.

**   "Religion, Crime and Citizens' Rights: A Dialogue on Tibet (II)," Beijing Review, October 26-November 1, 1987, p. 25.

express themselves in favor of Tibetan independence, are to be considered criminals: "...separatist activities and efforts made to undermine the unification of the motherland are violations of the law and will be dealt with in accordance with judicial procedures."*

Such statements represent dissimulation on the part of the authorities; an attempt to avoid the question of political imprisonment. So too, in denying reports of Lobsang Wangchuk's death in prison, one official spokesman went so far as to say that such a person was not even being held! The asserted basis for this denial lay with the fact that prior to his arrest in 1981 he had been imprisoned for participation in the 1959 uprising in Lhasa. Thus, the spokesman insisted, "This information is completely false, since all prisoners arrested after the 1959 uprising have been released."**

Along similar lines, the Panchen Lama recently stated in an article published in China that:

> [A]ny country that ensures "human rights" also has its laws, and it is impermissible to break them. The Constitution of China clearly stipulates that "Tibet is an integral part of China." Any attempt at "Tibetan Independence" is an attempt to split the country, and therefore unconstitutional....In its amendment on "Tibetan human rights," the United States Congress calls Losang Wangjiu [=Lobsang Wangchuk], a "political prisoner," a "prisoner of conscience." Actually, he was tried and sentenced several years ago by the Lhasa People's Court for secessionary activities. In 1985...he wrote to me admitting to me that he had broken the law and expressing his regrets and repentance.***

---

* "Our Differences with the Dalai Lama: A Dialogue on Tibet (I)," Beijing Review, October 19, 1987, p. 15.

** "Death of Leading Tibetan Activist Denied," FBIS-CHI-87-225, November 23, 1987, quoting an Agence France-Presse dispatch of November 22, 1987.

*** "Panchen Lama on 'Tibetan Independence'," China Reconstructs, January 1988, p. 15.

(In spite of these comments we note that all information available to Asia Watch concerning Lobsang Wangchuk and his case make the change of heart described by the Panchen Lama appear unlikely.)

Allegations of political imprisonment and mistreatment of prisoners are thus brushed aside by PRC authorities. The concerns and criticisms raised in the United States and elsewhere over the last several months are generally avoided with simple admonitions to interlocutors to more or less mind their own business. The Chinese position is generally articulated as follows:

> On 18 June, the U.S. House of Representatives approved [an amendment on] "infringement by the People's Republic of China upon human rights in Xizang [= Tibet]," arbitrarily vilifying China....[T]he U.S. Congress interferes in other countries' internal affairs under the banner of "protecting human rights." As everyone is aware, human rights are not abstract, and manifest themselves in a different manner with different countries and systems. As to how a citizen of a country should enjoy his rights, these are utterly internal affairs of the country, and no other country has the right to interfere.*

> ...[T]he affairs of Xizang are totally internal affairs of China. The Dalai Lama has attempted to restore the brutal serf system so that people in Tibet will return to the abyss of suffering. [U.S. Congressman] Lantos accuses China of violating human rights in Xizang. Does he think that only by the restoration of the serf system can the people in Xizang enjoy their human rights?**

> Some U.S. Congressmen are not diligent in sweeping away the snow in front of their doors. They are fond of paying attention to the frost on the roof of other people's houses. They have

---

* "Paper Views U.S. Congress' 'Interference,'" CHI July 23, 1987, p. B2, quoting an article in Zhongguo fazhi bao, July 3, 1987, by Xuan Yu entitled (in English translation) "Moves Running Counter to International Law — Recently the U.S. Congress Interfered Successfully in Other Countries' Internal Affairs."

** "Embassy Condemns Lantos," FBIS-CHI-87-223, November 19, 1987, p. 3, quoting a report from Hong Kong's Zhongguo xinwen she, put out on November 18, 1987.

their own purpose, of course: They throw mud on other people's faces to make their own faces look particularly white. Concerning human rights, people will ask these gentlemen: What kind of human rights do you want in Xizang? The "human rights" of serf owners in former times to take out their serf's eyes and to cut off their noses, hands, and feet?*

This criticism is of course not limited to U.S. officials. Confronting Han Xu, the Chinese ambassador to the U.S., an American who had been in Lhasa during the September and October demonstrations brought up the Tibetan issue and said "There are human rights violations that you have to acknowledge," to which the envoy replied "First you look into your own affairs...[t]hen you poke your head into the affairs of others."**

More recently, in response to the passage by both houses of Congress on December 15 and 16, 1987 of an amendment criticizing human rights violations in Tibet, the Nationalities Committee and the Foreign Affairs Committee of China's National People's Congress issued a statement that said in part:

> Anyone familiar with Tibetan history knows that under the previous dark rule of serfdom, the serfs and slaves who accounted for over 95 per cent of the Tibetan population were faring worse that beasts of burden, with no freedom of person, let alone "human rights." Only after the democratic reform in Tibet [1959] did the Tibetan people become real masters of their own destiny. Today they exercise their full rights as masters. Every basic right of the Tibetan people is protected by law and fully respected in actual life. The Tibetan people have never before enjoyed such full and extensive democracy and freedom as they do today. The practice of democracy and the legal system in Tibet are being further improved. There are no such cases as arrest and execution in Tibet on account of religious beliefs....While raising the so-called issue of protecting "human rights" in Tibet the "amendment" supports

---

* "U.S. Congress 'Making an Uproar' Over Xizang," FBIS-CHI-87-231, December 2, 1987, p. 4, quoting an article in Renmin ribao on the same day.

** "2 Clash on Tibet, China," The Ithaca Journal, November 19, 1987.

the Dalai clique in its efforts to restore serfdom in Tibet. What on earth is this logic? Does it mean that restoration of serfdom conforms with the principles of "human rights?"*

The same statement also took up the question of Chinese migration into Tibet and in a rare statement of principle (while still maintaining that the number of Chinese in the TAR is only somewhat over 70,000) noted that "people of Han and other fraternal nationalities in China are completely justified in going to Tibet to help their Tibetan compatriots in socialist construction."**

* * *

Regrettably, the foregoing remarks make it plain that we are hard-pressed to establish with the Chinese authorities even the basis for a dialogue on human rights questions as they apply to Tibet. Ultimately, however, China's leaders and representatives in the U.S. and elsewhere will have to come to an understanding of the legitimacy of international concern in matters of human rights. This is not an issue that will simply go away if journalists are barred from Lhasa, nor is it an issue involving only a small number of U.S. Congressmen. It is no longer as easy as it once was to sweep matters such as political imprisonment and torture under the rug with a "mind your own business" attitude. The situation in Tibet will not be turned into a non-issue through silence and secrecy.

---

*　　"'Text' of Committees' Protest Against U.S.," FBIS-CHI-87-248, December 28, 1987, p. 4, quoting a Xinhua dispatch of December 26, 1987.

**　　"'Text' of Committees' Protest Against U.S.," FBIS-CHI-87-248, December 28, 1987, p.4, quoting a Xinhua dispatch of December 26, 1987.

ASIA WATCH'S POSITION AND RECOMMENDATIONS

Asia Watch believes that the prevalence of serious human rights abuses in Tibet is beyond dispute. The various matters that have been detailed in this report — restrictions on freedom of expression and assembly, political imprisonment, secret trials, the mistreatment of political prisoners — all are part of a system of repression in Tibet that violates accepted international norms of respect for human rights.

It does not do to assert that such abuses are beyond the bounds of discussion for those outside China's borders; the world we live in today makes that an antiquated argument. Nor does it do for PRC spokesmen to hark back to the alleged evils of pre-1950 Tibet as justification for present practices. We live in the 1980s and we deal with problems and questions of the 1980s; no one seriously suggests that the only alternative to present practices in Tibet is the institution of arbitrary eye-gouging and amputations. The alternative must lie in the cessation of secret trials, political imprisonment, torture, discriminatory practices, and other violations of basic human rights.

It does not do either to treat the outcry over the situation in Tibet as simple interference in China's internal affairs by meddling U.S. Congressmen. Little has been done by the U.S. government beyond discussion, debate, and the passage of congressional resolutions. The Administration, moreover, has adopted an approach that seems designed to quiet U.S. criticism on the question rather than to deal with the substance of those concerns. The fact is that human rights violations in Tibet have become a concern for many in the U.S. and elsewhere. They are not the oratorical domain of a few American Congressmen.

Asia Watch finds that a number of internationally accepted standards of human rights are knowingly violated by the authorities in Tibet. These include provisions of the Universal Declaration of Human Rights, such as freedom from torture or cruel and inhuman punishment (article 5); freedom from arbitrary arrest (article 9); freedom of thought, conscience and religion (article 18); freedom of opinion and expression (article 19); and freedom of assembly (article 20).

Asia Watch is also very concerned about the environment of discrimination that marks many Tibetan cities and towns, where new Chinese populations are appearing. In this regard it is pertinent to point out that China acceded to the International Convention on the Elimination of All Forms of Racial Discrimination in December 1981. The inequalities in housing, education, and job opportunities that have been described earlier stand in violation of the provisions of the convention.

Article 1 defines racial discrimination as:

any distinction, exclusion, restriction or preference based on race, color, descent, or national or ethnic origins which has the purpose or effect of nullifying or impairing the recognition, enjoyment or exercise, on an equal footing, of human rights and fundamental freedoms in the political, economic, social, cultural and any other field of public life.

Article 5 of the Convention reiterates many of the rights enumerated in the Universal Declaration of Human Rights, but adds that these rights are to be enjoyed without racial or national distinctions. The same article enjoins all signatories to respect certain social and cultural rights, including the rights to work and to just and favorable conditions of work; the right to housing; and the right to education and training. All of these, according to the covenant, must be respected without any reference to racial or national differences.

These remarks ought to make it clear that human rights violations in Tibet cannot be considered solely as an internal affair of the PRC. The adoption of international conventions on human rights bears witness to the fact that human rights is a global concern. In acceding to the International Convention on the Elimination of All Forms of Racial Discrimination, the PRC undertook to respect its provisions. That it is not doing so is sufficient cause for expressing concern both inside and outside the PRC.

* * *

In 1987, the Reagan Administration continued its diplomatic and economic rapprochement with the PRC. But in its rush to court this world power, the Administration played down the seriousness of the situation in Tibet. The Administration thus failed to capitalize on the PRC government's strong desire for improved ties with the West by linking such ties to progress on the human rights front and by vigorously protesting abuses.

The Reagan Administration's initial reaction to the events of late September and early October was to voice support for the PRC government's effort to restore its authority in Tibet. The Administration also criticized an amendment, passed unanimously by the U.S. Senate, which condemned the Chinese government's actions.

On October 14, the Administration appeared to modify its stance when J. Stapleton Roy, Deputy Assistant Secretary of State for East Asian and Pacific Affairs, told two House Subcommittees:

> We cannot condone the use of weapons by public security authorities against unarmed demonstrations. We believe in the right of free and peaceful expression. When the Chinese expelled foreign journalists from Lhasa, U.S. diplomatic representatives in Lhasa made representations on their behalf.

Roy went on to support the Dalai Lama's call for "fundamental human rights and democratic freedoms" in Tibet, as well as the spiritual leader's demand that "Tibetan people must once again be free to develop culturally, intellectually, economically and spiritually, and to exercise strong democratic freedoms."* While the support for human rights in Tibet and the condemnation of the violence was welcome, it was too little and too late, coming as it did after much blood had been shed. Moreover, following the hearing, the Administra-

---

* Department of State Statement of Ambassador J. Stapleton Roy, Deputy Assistant Secretary of State, Bureau of East Asian and Pacific Affairs, Before the House Foreign Affairs Subcommittees on Human Rights and International Organizations and Asian and Pacific Affairs: "When the Dalai Lama states, as he did in his remarks to the Congressional Human Rights Caucus, that 'fundamental human rights and democratic freedoms must be respected in Tibet,' the Administration is in full agreement with him. When he states, as he did in his remarks, that 'Tibetan people must once again be free to develop culturally, intellectually, economically and spiritually and to exercise basic democratic freedoms,' the Administration is in full accord with his sentiments."

tion reverted to a stance of passive tolerance as it remained all but silent as political arrests continued in Tibet. This silence calls into question Roy's pledge that "the U.S. government will continue to do all it can to ensure respect for the dignity of man and individual human rights, in China as elsewhere."

In conclusion, Asia Watch is concerned that U.S. reluctance to condemn abuses against demonstrators calling for Tibetan independence may be due in part to U.S. recognition of Chinese sovereignty over Tibet. We strongly believe that all people have the elementary right to express themselves freely, and in a nonviolent manner, on political questions. Moreover, the human rights provisions of U.S. law require that U.S. officials promote those rights, *even when opinons expressed do not accord with U.S. policy*. In China, as elsewhere, freedom of expression is put to the test *only* when dissenting views are aired. It would be a grave error for the U.S. government to maintain its silence now, and to acquiesce in China's moves to throw a veil over events in Tibet. A stronger stand is required, and it is required now.

MEMBERS AND STAFF
OF THE
ASIA WATCH

Members

Jack Greenberg, Chairman; Matthew Nimetz, Aryeh Neier, Vice Chairmen; Floyd Abrams, Edward J. Baker, Robert L. Bernstein, Tom A. Bernstein, Julie Brill, Clarence Dias, Adrian DeWind, Dolores A. Donovan, Timothy A. Gelatt, Adrienne Germain, Merle Goldman, Deborah M. Greenberg, David Hawk, Liang Heng, Jeri Laber, Virginia Leary, Amit Pandya, Dith Pran, Stephen A. Rickard, Sheila Rothman, Barnett Rubin, James Scott, Judith Shapiro, Sophie C. Silberberg, Nadine Strossen

Staff

Eric Schwartz, Program Director and Counsel to Asia Watch; Holly Burkhalter, Washington Representative; Susan Osnos, Press Director; Jenny Jones, Ji Won Park, Associates

Publications of the
ASIA WATCH

Afghanistan:
"By All Parties to the Conflict: Violations of the Laws of War in Afghanistan," March 1988, 90 pages, $8.00, ISBN 0-938579-58-4

"To Die in Afghanistan," December 1985, 105 pages, $8.00 (Helsinki Watch/ Asia Watch) ISBN 0-938579-99-1

China:
"Intellectual Freedom in China: An Update," July 1985, 55 pages, $5.00 (Asia Watch/Fund for Free Expression) ISBN 0-938579-48-7

Indonesia:
"Human Rights Concerns in Indonesia," April 1986, 31 pages, $3.00

Korea:
"A Stern, Steady Crackdown: Legal Process and Human Rights in South Korea," May 1987, 133 pages

"Human Rights in Korea," January 1986, 364 pages, $15.00 ISBN 0-938579-74-6

Sri Lanka:
"Cycles of Violence: Human Rights in Sri Lanka Since the Indo-Sri Lanka Agreement," November 1987, 131 pages, ISBN 0-938579-43-6

Taiwan:
"Human Rights in Taiwan 1986-87," December 1987, 269 pages, $12.00, ISBN 0-938579-70-3

"Elections in Taiwan, December 6, 1986: Rules of the Game for the 'Democratic Holiday,'" November 1986, 71 pages, $5.00

"Human Rights in Taiwan," March 1987, 200 pages, $10.00, ISBN 0-938579-73-8

Vietnam:
"Still Confined: Journalists in 'Re-Education' Camps and Prisons in Vietnam," April 1987, 84 pages, $6.00, ISBN 0-938579-72-X

Human Rights Policies:
"The Persecution of Human Rights Monitors, December 1986 to December 1987, A Worldwide Survey, December 1987, 107 pages, $7.00, Human Rights Watch, ISBN 0-938579-44-4

"The Reagan Administration's Record on Human Rights in 1987," December 1987, 210 pages. $12.00 (Lawyers Committee for Human Rights/Human Rights Watch) ISBN 0-938579-42-8